nature of work

The new story of work for a living age

Paul Miller and **Shimrit Janes**

tecl
PUBLISHING

tecl
PUBLISHING

First published 2021

Published in the United Kingdom and United States by TECL Publishing, 30 City Road, London EC1Y 2AB, United Kingdom.

Paul Miller – Shimrit Janes
Nature of Work: The new story of work for a living age
1st edition, 2021
ISBN: 978-1-8381422-0-9
www.natureofwork.com

Copyediting and photography research by Alison Chapman

Design, typesetting and eBook by Mark Williams, Toast Design: www.toastdesign.co.uk

Woodland
CARBON
www.woodlandcarbon.co.uk
HOLYWELL PRESS LTD
14039900282
Printed on Carbon Captured paper

Printed and bound by Holywell Press, Oxford (holywellpress.com). The material used to produce this book has been carbon captured, helping to plant new native woodland across the UK through the Woodland Trust.

Digital Workplace Group

Digital Workplace Group (DWG) is a strategic partner, covering all aspects of the evolving digital workplace industry through membership, benchmarking and consultancy services. DWG provides expert advice, peer connections, research and insights to guide and support organizations globally on their journey towards digital workplace success.
www.digitalworkplacegroup.com

We delight in the beauty of the butterfly, but rarely admit the changes it has gone through to achieve that beauty.

Maya Angelou

Language is very powerful. Language does not just describe reality. Language creates the reality it describes.

Desmond Tutu

nature
of work

The new story of work
for a living age

Paul Miller and **Shimrit Janes**

tecl
PUBLISHING

London and New York

Acknowledgements

Conceiving, writing and producing a book that attempts to present a new story of work for a living age is far from a solo or even duo effort. *Nature of Work* has only been made possible due to the support and work of a very wide range of people who have all played a significant part.

Firstly, our extraordinary text and imagery editor, Alison Chapman, who brought ideas, direction, beauty and structure to what began as a nascent idea of work as a natural system. Then the ever patient and diligent Steve Bynghall, our research lead, who found stories and examples to cogently illuminate the sometimes esoteric concepts within. In the background have been DWG colleagues Elizabeth Marsh, critic and source of encouragement, insightfully reviewing and refining our drafts, and Lindsey Garner, who has so efficiently steered us through the production and distribution process.

We would like to thank Manisha Singh and Charles Eisenstein for kindly reading and reviewing the book to provide the Foreword and Afterword, and all the experts interviewed for the book, including Ryan Anderson, Morgane Bradley, Isabel de Clercq, Dianna Langley, Dr Nicola Millard and Florin Rotar.

A big thank you as well to Mark Williams of Toast Design for creating the beautiful look of this book and Holywell Press for their printing expertise.

Then, Barbara Eastman (our proofreader) and Susan Leech (our indexer), plus Kate Algar, Faye Andrews, Helen Day, Nancy Goebel, Anthony Gresford, Liad Janes, Rose Miller and Alison Newman, who have all contributed in important ways at different points in the process. A special mention too for the wonderful environment and staff of the Fish Hotel, near Broadway, UK, where some of the book was written. Thank you also to all the photographers and illustrators whose wonderful imagery brings our ideas to life. And finally, to the many people we spoke to during the inception and writing of this book, from DWG members and clients, to friends and family, too countless to name, but all of whom have played a crucial role in helping us to shape our ideas.

Authors

Paul Miller is a technology and social entrepreneur. He is CEO and Founder of Digital Workplace Group (DWG), rated by the *Financial Times* in 2020 as one of the UK's leading management consultancies in digital transformation. His previous books include *The Digital Renaissance of Work: Delivering digital workplaces fit for the future* (co-authored with Elizabeth Marsh), which was shortlisted for the Management Book of the Year 2016 Award, and *The Digital Workplace: How technology is liberating work*, which helped to popularize the term 'digital workplace'.

Paul lives in the Cotswolds in the UK and is a keen tennis player and long-time yoga practitioner.

Shimrit Janes is Director of Knowledge for DWG, focused on curating knowledge on the digital workplace for its members and clients such as Adobe, The Coca-Cola Company, Ubisoft and UNHCR. She has worked with Paul and DWG colleagues on various initiatives, such as Digital Nations Group, as well as co-hosting the 24-hour global digital experience DWG24. She has had a number of research papers published with DWG on topics such as organizational readiness and collaboration.

Shimrit lives in London, where she crochets, enjoys video games and keeps more books than the space allows.

Additional content

Research on *Nature of Work* was supported by **Steve Bynghall**. Steve is an independent digital workplace consultant and writer. He has been Research and Knowledge Lead at DWG for over a decade. Based in London, Steve is a prolific author in the digital workplace space and has contributed to several books.

Contents

Nature Of Work

Nature Of Work Elements

Reflections on Nature Of Work

Nature Of Work Details

Foreword

Manisha Singh
Vice President, Digital and People Experience
AstraZeneca

"The best way to predict your future is to create it."

Peter Drucker

My personal mission in life and at work is to design a future that loves us all.

The word 'design' in this statement says that we have the power to shape our future rather than to be passive recipients of what unfolds. My deliberate inclusion of 'love' speaks of a world with a place for all, with diverse individuals, organizations, communities and societies.

This decade, the 2020s, which Paul Miller and Shimrit Janes call the 'Decade of Courage', is a call to determined change-makers, transformation leaders, sustainability champions, visionary C-Suite executives and my fellow HR leaders to be **bold** and to seize this remarkable and challenging moment in history.

I have worked for 20 years to help create fair, equitable and just workplaces, which unleash the infinite potential within every individual and, through that, of the organization and our wider societies. We now have a window in time to define the world of work of the future, for generations to come, as we rethink and redefine what the new normal, resilient, adaptable and agile organization will be.

Paul and Shimrit have shown us in their revolutionary book that there are 12 elements that can inspire a deeper way of harnessing collective intelligence and activating a connected intention to grow, adapt and thrive.

They have described and illustrated a world of work that is living and natural.

This book steers us through multidisciplinary concepts and examples, drawing from biology, anthropology, design and organization development to connect the dots. These powerful stories will yield disproportionate dividends for us collectively.

As I write, COVID-19 has accelerated the debate about digital transformation, digital workplace movement and flexibility by a decade, and my hope is that this book will help to propel forward the future of work conversation by a century.

As an enterprise leader for people experiences and digital transformation, I have found it inspiring and useful to read the new language in this book about how to design, nurture and cultivate the nested ecosystem of living and working experiences. Our habitats allow diverse teams, networks and individuals to grow, adapt, regenerate and harness intelligence to realize their dreams and hopes.

For any leader seeking to build a sustainable organization and to humanize work and workforce experiences, *Nature of Work* is a seminal piece of work that creates a compelling metaphor to enable truly healthy growth and collective conscience in any company, working community or organization.

Welcome to Nature of Work

"We hope Nature of Work will become more of a shared movement than a pre-set blueprint."

Your organization and the world of work in which you spend so much of your life are alive.

For years, decades, centuries even, we have behaved as though this wasn't the case. We have acted as if organizations and work are machines: mechanistic systems that can be programmed down to the last cog or circuit board. And in approaching our organizations as machines, we have treated the people who work within them likewise as parts of those machines. Clock in. Clock out. Leave your feelings at the door. Be efficient. Get the job done.

While this mindset has spurred huge growth and riches for many, it's an approach that has masked a fundamental truth:

Rather than a machine, your organization is a living, dynamic system that can't be programmed. Instead, it thrives through relationships, adaptive structures, diverse networks of people, the spaces they occupy, the tools they use, the knowledge and intelligence they pulsate with – and so, so much more.

It's a community of people, working together and seeking to achieve great things that as individuals they couldn't dream of doing alone, with no one day exactly the same as the day before – because *we* aren't exactly the same today as we were yesterday.

We think, we feel, we hurt, we play. Together, we are the organizations within which we work. The decisions we make, the challenges we face, the things we create and those we destroy define us.

So, what story should we use to describe this living system of work and its elements? What language can we create to allow us to start to talk about it and think about it in new and different ways? How can we break away from the language and story of industrialization inherited from generations past, and evolve forward in our own way?

For us – Paul and Shimrit and DWG – the answer is **Nature of Work**: a new language inspired by forests and other elements of the natural world. This new vocabulary helps us to perceive work in a more dynamic way; to move away from the 'organization as machine' model and towards an 'organization as organism' view.

As our species, along with the many other creatures with whom we share the planet Earth, face ever more complex challenges and crises, whether through the climate emergency, global pandemics or social injustices, the language and stories of nature can help us better understand ourselves, each other and this whole world on which we all so deeply rely and so profoundly impact.

This is Nature of Work. And through these pages, we invite you to embark on this journey towards a more natural understanding of your working world, not alone, but together with us. And, in this way, to see your own working life, as well as that of your colleagues, in a new light: this is no longer the industrial age, or even the digital age, but the living age.

When we look at the complexity, patterns and beauty in nature, we can see the model for new ways of working and organizing.

The Golden Ratio is a special number (1.618) with a related mathematical pattern (the Golden Spiral) found widely across nature, in the shapes of shells, plants, hurricanes and even galaxies. The unique proportions of both have inspired artists, architects and designers over centuries, influencing the design of anything from the Parthenon and Da Vinci's Vitruvian Man right through to modern-day logos and web pages.[1,2]

How to use this book

Why a book with images of nature?

We've deliberately designed this book not to look like a 'normal' business book, but instead to resemble a coffee table book about nature. New language and ways of seeing can challenge us to think differently and, in this respect, the medium is just as important as the message.

And so, throughout this book, you'll find carefully selected images and photographs from the natural world that have inspired us and moved us as we've conducted our research and our writing. We hope they motivate you too to think about your own work differently.

Our disclaimer up front is that neither of us is a natural history expert (or even a gifted amateur!), so while we have done our best to provide accurate statements on the natural world and reference our sources, we apologize in advance if any of our observations do not stand up to full academic scrutiny. Our justification is that we are not trying to write a scientific book about forests or animal behaviour but rather to use the natural world as inspiration – as a signifier and metaphor for how organizations could experience themselves.

How is this book structured?

We first explore what Nature of Work is, and why it's so important for us all to start thinking about our work and our organizations in this way.

We have then structured the remainder of the book into 12 elements drawn from the natural world, which are mapped against aspects of organizational life.

These elements are:
- Purpose
- Roots
- Habitats
- Biodiversity
- Relationships
- Structures
- Life cycles
- Migration
- Threats
- Regeneration
- Intelligence
- Health

For each element we include:
- Definitions of the element in relation to nature and to work.
- Examples from the natural world related to the element.
- How the element connects back to the world of work and what this reveals to us about work.
- Real-life examples of organizations already working in this way, as well as insights from practitioners, experts and thought leaders with notable quotes. These appear as 'biomarkers' throughout the book, inspired by the use of biomarkers in science and medicine as measurable indicators of health states and conditions. The biomarkers are headed with either a leaf (*thought leadership*), a flower (*inspiring practices*) or a spiral (*examples from nature*).
- Questions to ask yourself when working through what this element means for your work and for your organization or work community.

The Cologne Oval Offices in Germany echo their Rhine River location, drawing on patterns in nature to create space for a natural world of work. The whole building is designed with energy efficiency in mind with groundwater from the Rhine running both heating and cooling systems.

Why has this been written by DWG?

It seems hard to believe now but, a little over a decade ago, the notion of the 'digital workplace' was entirely new. DWG's sector-defining book, *The Digital Workplace: How technology is liberating work*[3], explored in depth for the first time the concept of there being two parallel but intertwined spaces of work: the physical and the digital. The book proposed that all work happens in either one or the other – but most often in both spaces simultaneously.

With this writing, the first seeds of a new language that would define and explain the rapidly emerging technology-enabled, human-centred world of work had been planted. It was a new story for the then nascent industry, which is now – just 12 years later – worth more than $30 billion a year and growing fast.[4] Out of this different way of looking at work was also born our own organization, Digital Workplace Group (DWG), in a metamorphosis from its original adolescent form, Intranet Benchmarking Forum.

But, just like DWG, language and work evolve. While the term 'digital workplace' still remains valuable in describing and defining digital worlds of work, it has its limitations. The digital workplace tends to be perceived as a collection of technologies in varying levels of fragmentation or integration – a rather clinical, technical summation of work.

Even the concept of the human-centred digital world of work can exclude a raft of key qualities and experiences that significantly impact and shape work in the 2020s. Other new terminology and models that have emerged, such as 'employee experience', are all useful but limited in their own ways too. Areas such as where we work, the nature of offices, culture, relationships, wellbeing, diversity, innovation, location and demographics, to name but a few, are all critical to our experience of work, but seemingly so far lack a shared language that allows us to talk about them in unison.

From the early stages of 2019, in DWG we were beginning to seek to understand and describe another new story of work that we were starting to see emerge around us. Over the past year or so, we've been talking about the concept 'Nature of Work' in research reports, podcasts and presentations.[1] This book is the natural next step for us in exploring these ideas in more depth.

We know that we are not experts in all 12 elements of work covered here; our day-to-day focus is as a global consulting, research and membership company, specializing in the digital world of work. Our main purpose is to help organizations and work communities handle the challenges and opportunities at the points where humans, technology (soon to include biology) and work meet.

We seek to think forward about the Nature of Work, and in doing so to challenge both ourselves and you, the reader, to think about work and organizations in this new way too.

Who is this book for?

Our belief is that, while the readership of this book will be wide-ranging in terms of role, seniority, age and geography, the common thread at its core will be what can best be described as 'change-makers' in work.

These are people who, whether in a role inside an organization or working independently, want to make a real difference in their world of work – people who want to leave a mark and make their organizations better.

So, all you change-makers, engage with this book, be intrigued by it – and challenge yourselves! Read it more than once if needed, share it around, discuss it with your colleagues, with your friends and with your families.

Create your own change plan

We want to help you create your own change plan, and so we've posed questions to ask yourself at the end of each section to empower you to consider how the elements relate to you personally, and what they mean for you as a change-maker in your different roles and spheres of influence. Interact with the content; note how it makes you think and feel by jotting down ideas as they occur to you and writing down your answers to the questions.

The book, *Nature of Work*, is not meant to be a 'how to' guide; it tells a new story of work and can be used in a variety of ways such as to:

- Challenge yourself about how you conceptualize and approach work.

- Start conversations with colleagues in your organization or work community.
- Seek to influence senior leaders.
- Engage likeminded co-workers in a working group.
- Do something outside the organization.
- Join in relevant forums externally, such as speaking at events.

We hope the concept Nature of Work will become more of a shared movement than a pre-set blueprint. For us, this is a collective initiation – something akin to what many societies or mythology might call a 'rite of passage' – into a new way of working and organizing.

If this proves to be correct, then, as others like you join the movement and begin to view their organizations as alive, practices, plans and roadmaps will undoubtedly emerge. New language will surface and terms arrive as we move from the machine concept to the experience of ourselves as a living system. Either way, we can all share via the online platforms where we work and through the channels we are launching alongside this book. On this journey we all need to encourage each other.

So, pause now to take a deep breath. Get ready to embark on this voyage of exploration with us, and prepare to move yourself and your organization from machine to living system, as part of the new Nature of Work for our living age.

Why Nature of Work?

"The global pandemic revealed just how connected we all are and how work doesn't exist in the closed environment of the individual organization but seeps into every aspect of the human experience."

Brutal lessons

Our writing on this book began in 2019, some six months before COVID-19 was announced officially as a global pandemic by the World Health Organization. The world in which we finished writing the book wasn't the same as the one in which we had begun.

Among its numerous impacts, one of the effects of the pandemic was to put 'work' itself in the spotlight as never before. It brought home how far-reaching work is in its impact on people's quality of life, the environment, and also the extent to which the structure of our society depends upon it. It revealed just how connected we all are and how work doesn't exist in the closed environment of the individual organization but seeps into every aspect of the human experience. All the services and products we rely on every day are a consequence of other people's work, and we ourselves each create services or products on which others rely.

In a strange, completely unforeseen, worldwide 'experiment' in remote working, we saw a dramatic shift within days, sometimes hours, to hyper-distributed – and, in many cases, *home* – working for large swathes of the global workforce. This in itself highlighted the different nature of people's work, which often comes down to those who are able to work from anywhere and those who aren't.

Nature's ability to repair

We saw too that when we change where we work and how we work, a raft of significant consequential effects flow. The dramatic reduction in business and work-related travel played a central role in revealing nature's ability to respond and regenerate; for example, the Himalayan mountains of Nepal became visible from New Delhi in India for the first time in decades (*see opposite*).[5]

We heard countless stories of workers saying their work/life balance had been transformed by not having to do the daily commute. Large organizations shut down city-centre office buildings and started to explore the possibility of shared workspaces closer to where people live. At the same time, economies and livelihoods that had spun up around the daily commute came under threat – and in many cases now face extinction.

Questions around what was considered 'essential' or 'key' work created a divide between those who could work from home, those who had to stop working temporarily or altogether, and those who needed to be present in particular locations, such as hospitals or supermarkets. And the impact of unpaid labour, such as caregiving and housework, also came under scrutiny as the home/work divide became blurred in more intense ways, disproportionately impacting women's ability to undertake paid work.[6]

What we now know is that when we change the ecosystem of work, the world shifts too – and fast. COVID-19 turned work (and everything else) upside down, transforming our understanding of work forever in ways we are still (as we write in mid-2020) discovering. Tragically, in too many cases, our insight that organizations are really 'organisms' – not machines but living systems – has been shown to be only too true, in many cases demonstrated as a biting, harsh reality.

Himalayan mountains, Jammu and Kashmir, India. As a result of early 2020 COVID-19 travel restrictions, the Kailash Kund range was visible from as far away as 200km for the first time in decades. Sustained reductions in work travel may help reduce global pollution levels.

And so, while we revised this book 'in flight' in response to the unforeseen effects of the COVID-19 experience and the ways in which the virus forced such dramatic changes to where and how we work, at its core the central premise has changed little, if anything bringing it into even sharper focus.

The need for fundamental shifts in how we comprehend work as alive and organizations as interconnected living systems, pre-dates and will outlive the pandemic. The relevance of this conversation about how to transform how we work, where we work and what work means, has just been emphatically strengthened by the global health crisis.

Language creates reality

Societies across the globe have the possibility of transitioning to a new work age, in which we collectively evolve a better understanding of the demands and requirements of work, and the interconnectedness of work with the multiple further connected aspects of society and the natural world.

However, this transition won't be possible if we continue to envisage work through the lens we have employed ever since the industrial age. Instead, new language, new models and new mindsets will be needed.

One interesting illustration of how language can effect change occurs in the 2016 science fiction film *Arrival*. Linguist Dr Louise Banks (played by Amy Adams) and physicist Ian Donnelly (Jeremy Renner) discover that alien visitors who are being monitored in different locations around the world haven't 'arrived' to destroy humanity, as had been suspected. Instead, they're here to bequeath to humankind an entirely new, highly complex language that, once understood, will unlock unprecedented levels of global cooperation and interdependence.[7]

In a neat plot twist, we discover that the motivation for this act of generosity is not just to give *Homo sapiens* a much needed helping hand. It's also because, being an advanced species (and time travellers too, of course), the aliens know that at some future date they will need our help to save their own species – and it would surely be rude of us not to then repay the favour!

In this film, the new language creates the possibility of greater connection and interbeing – and without new language to describe fresh realities, we remain stuck in the same patterns and mindset as our ancestors.

The persistence of a mechanistic worldview

We know that 'work' is underpinned by a complex web of relationships and connections, where decisions, actions and events all impact the health, not only of organizations as entities in themselves, but also of their people, of communities, of societies, and ultimately of our shared planet.

And yet, despite the complexity inherent in the ecosystem of work, much of how we think and talk about work today has its roots in a mechanistic worldview and language born during the industrial era.

It's with relative ease that we can look to that industrial age, which emerged in the 18th century in Western civilisations,

Rita Gunther McGrath writes in the *Harvard Business Review*: 'Organization as machine – this imagery from our industrial past continues to cast a long shadow over the way we think about management today.'[8]

Arie de Geus remembers his first experience of work after business school as one of disconnection between work theory and reality: 'Soon after I walked in the door (of the Shell refinery near Rotterdam) I felt a slight level of discomfort. The theories back in business school had mentioned labour, but there had been no talk of people. Yet the real world, the refinery, seemed to be full of them. And because the workplace was full of people, it looked surprisingly as if companies were not always rational, calculable and controllable.'[9]

and see that much of the way we view work today stems from beliefs and practices forged among the often appalling conditions found in the factories, coalmines, cotton fields and dense city dwellings that were intrinsic to industry. Those practices derived from an overarching emphasis on efficiency and measurement, driven by the prevailing focus on outputs, inputs and productivity.

But there was something missing in those calculations, a key factor that would later be glimpsed in the self-organization of workers demanding more rights, in their strikes calling for better conditions, and in the eventual emergence of labour laws and unions.

The Industrial Revolution was powered by people; not the few who held sway at the top of the hierarchy, but by the 'working classes' who toiled in the factories and mills, and, even more traumatically, by the many who were transported far away from their homelands in Africa as slaves.

All these people were reduced to being viewed and treated as mere 'parts' of a wider industrial machine that churned out products for selling and consumption, resulting in a sharp focus on output, management and profits. 'Labour' was but yet another resource in that supply chain.

The Industrial Revolution transitioned us from an agrarian economy (much closer to nature at the physical and community levels, although not without its undoubted inequities and often inhumane treatment) to the concept of the organization, company and particularly the limited liability company with its own legal identity.

The industrial age brought with it the narrative of work as duty, obligation and suffering, within work situations that were often, quite literally, toxic. And then, when the locations of manufacturing shifted to areas of cheaper labour, communities were frequently left without employment opportunities or investment, again causing harm.

Even though we have in large part transitioned out of the industrial era, that mechanistic experience of work persists, with its habits and patterns still in evidence all around us. This has, for instance, influenced how we categorize 'white-collar workers' in contrast to 'blue-collar workers', or define and think about 'knowledge workers' as opposed to people dubbed 'frontline workers' (as if these somehow work without knowledge!).

The mechanistic view is embedded in how we assess a person's performance, how we calculate productivity and how we seek to measure an organization's success. At the national level, we see countries defined in terms of gross domestic product (GDP), which asks purely what a nation produces and the financial value we can place on that, rather than how happy, satisfied and safe its people feel.

Quantitative and financial measures are important (albeit partial) indicators of overall 'health', but are far from capable of presenting a true picture of the health of an organizational system. A solely 'machine-led' story doesn't allow for conflict, love, fear, anxiety, joy, family, community, cooperation. It doesn't account for why people work, or what 'satisfying work' looks like.[11] And it doesn't attempt to gauge how work impacts not only our individual but also our

Peter Senge in his Foreword for Arie de Geus' *The Living Company* writes: 'I believe that almost all of us adopt the machine assumption without ever thinking about it… In so doing, we probably mould the destiny of individual organisations far more than we imagine… As Arie points out, the machine metaphor is so powerful that it shapes the character of most organisations. They have become more like machines than like living beings because their members think of them that way. So, perhaps our first mandate is to shift our thinking.'[9]

Giles Hutchins writes in his 2012 book, *The Nature of Business: Redesigning for resilience*: 'If these stories (about organization as machine) are taken for granted and never questioned, then they tend to be reproduced over and over again. The social and scientific revolutions in modern, early modern and even ancient ages have left their legacies with the modern mind, and ultimately the "stories" it unwittingly defaults to.'[10]

collective experiences of living.

And yet, this industrial, profit-driven view has remained an enduring and resilient perspective, even when we declared ourselves as having moved first into an 'information age' and more recently into what some, like PwC, are naming an 'age of purpose'.[12]

There are echoes of these inherited industrial-age legacies to be heard in reports about the rights and conditions of workers in factories, warehouses and within the gig economy. We can observe centuries-old ways of looking at things in how organizational cultures and leadership treat those they employ solely as numbers on a balance sheet – and we can all too often trace physical, emotional and psychological health, anxiety and stress effects back to the work situations of those experiencing such treatment.

This mechanistic story of work, where everything and everybody can seemingly be counted and managed has persisted even as it's become no longer fit for purpose – if it ever was. The implications for how we perceive and organize work are compelling.

From industrial age to living age

The Nature of Work view means releasing ourselves from these inherited industrialized cognitive models, to create and experience a new, holistic worldview of the role of work – not only within society, but also in relation to our planet, Earth.

We can take what we've learned and select what we wish to retain. We can regenerate, creating an understanding of what work can be

if it's released from its old 'story' and is instead allowed to flourish. We can already glimpse some fresh shoots in small, fertile patches: people in organizations acting with empathy, beginning to better understand the role they play in others' lives and the impact they have on wider society.

In the early days of the COVID-19 pandemic, stories emerged of organizations discovering new levels of empathy and compassion for their employees, suppliers, customers, clients and communities, comprehending more fully, maybe for the first time, the larger role these all play in their ecosystems. Others rapidly lost the trust of their people by putting profit before people.[13]

During the Black Lives Matter protests of 2020, we saw how some organizations were able to begin to recognize their role in the proliferation of systemic racism and their need for specific action. Others saw only an opportunity for a quick PR statement of support.[14]

What's more, the industrial model of power and advancement has come at huge costs to the natural world – and we are now experiencing the tragic consequences of our actions and norms. What seemed viable once, now seems like sheer stupidity and arrogance. We excavated the earth, removed its fossils and minerals, cut down the trees, plundering and pillaging in order to burn, meld and build however we saw fit. And after we had extracted all the 'value' we could from what had once been alive, to transport, entertain and house us, we took what we then no longer needed in its

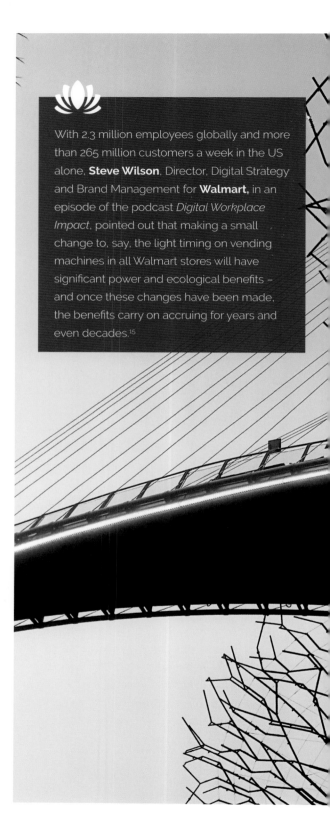

With 2.3 million employees globally and more than 265 million customers a week in the US alone, **Steve Wilson**, Director, Digital Strategy and Brand Management for **Walmart,** in an episode of the podcast *Digital Workplace Impact*, pointed out that making a small change to, say, the light timing on vending machines in all Walmart stores will have significant power and ecological benefits – and once these changes have been made, the benefits carry on accruing for years and even decades.[15]

Gardens by the Bay nature park, Singapore, part of the nation's plans to create a 'city in a garden' to enhance greenery in the city. There are positive wellbeing work effects where buildings 'mimic' nature in design.

In May 2020, **DWG** published the *Decade of Courage Manifesto* to provide a blueprint for organizations, with 12 key action points for that moment when the digital workplace became (almost overnight) the *essential* workplace, with large swathes of the working population required to work from home. The concept of the 2020s as a decade underpinned by courage had first been introduced by DWG in late 2019 in its end-of-year predictions. The manifesto discussed leadership empathy, radical shifts in work location, raising digital literacy and a digital focus on firstline/frontline staff. Courage derives from the French word 'coeur' meaning 'heart', embracing two strands: finding courage in ourselves and encouraging others to meet the challenges ahead.[16]

depleted state and deposited it back into the earth as what we casually describe as 'waste'.

Issues of environmental impact, ethics, morality, social justice and human rights demand answers and action from the people and decision-makers within organizations who have the power to enact change. Where once large companies acted as though they could operate in a kind of bubble, distinct from politics, social change and climate, in recent years this has become impossible due to customer and employee pressure for organizations to find their voice, recognize the role they play and take a clear position.

Organizations, both large and small, can begin by admitting what they have done, often deliberately, at other times unwittingly, in the relentless drive to feed our seemingly insatiable appetite for resources. Only once we've acknowledged the guilt and grief for what has been destroyed, can we start to heal and adapt. We have not for the most part been deliberately evil, but we have been ignorant and thoughtless on a huge scale and, as a result, have caused untold damage to our planet and to each other.

Decade of Courage

DWG has dubbed the 2020s the 'Decade of Courage'[16] and in this same pioneering and encouraging spirit, so this book calls for us all to view where, how and why we work as something alive, as an organism with its own innate vitality and even consciousness – not merely as a collection of people surrounded by tools and processes, but as vibrant communities harbouring (or at least longing for) a deep shared purpose.

As at 2019, there were 3.46 billion people working globally according to the World Bank[17], representing 41% of the world's population of all ages. Given these numbers, any changes in work can have a monumental impact on all aspects of life. And not only do these changes affect working people, they ripple out to affect all those who receive services or products as customers too. Changes in the world of work have profound impacts on how we live on Earth.

This is the era of the Nature of Work and this book offers a challenge for us all to think about work, its purpose and our place in it, in an integrated, dynamic and even beautiful way: to evolve from the language of the machine and industry towards a vocabulary based on organisms and ecosystems. We suggest that we must weave closer together the natural world with our human-made world, to find a way forward that works for all.

Ask yourself

- Have there been times when you've felt as if you've been treated more like a machine than a human being in your working life? What was the impact of that on you?
- How do you think about work, your organization or work community, and your colleagues? What parts of the old 'industrial' story are you carrying with you?
- Are there parts of that story which have been beneficial? And are there others that have been harmful?

What is Nature of Work?

"Humans have always sought to better understand themselves through telling stories."

You and your organization are alive

The way we experience work is different for each of us – why we work; our relationships with the people paying us to do it and with our colleagues; the way we feel about our job the night before having to get up for it the next morning or as we prepare for a night shift – all will vary hugely from person to person. How our work combines (or doesn't) with the time we spend *not* working is also often an area of strident debate and concern.

The living system through which work takes place is complex, intermingled with many different factors and, as we saw in 'Why Nature of Work?', bringing important ramifications for people's lives as well as the way in which society is structured.

In recent years, wellbeing programmes, flexible working arrangements, corporate social responsibility (CSR), and diversity and inclusion initiatives have started to emerge as approaches that acknowledge these more human elements of work. But these ways of thinking don't yet sit at the heart of organizations in terms of strategy, operations, key indicators of success and performance, or ultimately in relation to understanding the purpose of what the organization is for.

The closest we've come so far to better integrating this more sensitive approach to work is in areas such as systems thinking. Here, we can find frameworks, tools, methodologies and theories to help us see how the elements of a system are interconnected, emergent and complex.[18] This is also where we can notice the beginnings of a new, post-mechanistic story that will help us better visualize work and the organization as a living, dynamic system.

To understand the full ecosystem of work, we need to consider all the various and connected nested systems of which 'work' consists. A team is made up of individuals; a department or unit is a collection of teams; an organization is a work community housing multiple thriving, overlapping networks; society consists of multiple organizations. And so on.

Work is formed of an ever-changing, emergent web of people and their relationships, flows of ideas and knowledge, organizational culture, beliefs, values, intentions and behaviours – and what happens when these are all brought together. It impacts and is influenced by the natural environment, communities of people, families and economies. It teems with both unpredictability and structure. In essence, it is a living system.

A new (and ancient) story of work inspired by nature

Humans have always sought to better understand themselves through telling stories – and often stories derived from the natural world. Remarkably, evidence of our storytelling instinct reaches back to 30,000-year-old cave art, where an erupting volcano is depicted.[19]

Key devices for storytelling (for as long as there have been stories, it seems) have included analogy, metaphor and simile. Exploring how 'this' is like 'that' through a tale can be a powerful way of enabling a listener to attach their prior comprehension of a familiar kind of person, object or situation to one that is less familiar.

Scientists **Fritjof Capra** and **Pier Luigi Luisi**, in their 2014 book *The Systems View of Life*, wrote that, prior to 1500, the dominant worldview in most civilisations was organic: 'People lived in small, cohesive communities and experienced nature in terms of personal relationships' – their understanding of the world and human's place in it was intimately connected with their relationship with the natural world. But, from the 16th century on: 'The notion of an organic, living and spiritual universe was replaced by that of the world as machine, and the mechanistic conception of reality became the basis of the modern worldview.'

Capra and Luisi proposed a new understanding of biology and nature that supported a different comprehension of our place on Earth, within a more organic framework of living systems. They suggested that the modern roots of the living system notion can be found in 20th century biology, where biologists started to think about nature and organisms as only being fully comprehensible as a network of smaller parts within a larger whole: 'Each... forms a whole with respect to its parts while at the same time being part of a larger whole. Thus, cells combine to form tissues, tissues to form organs, and organs to form organisms. These in turn exist within social systems and ecosystems. Throughout the living world, we find living systems nesting within other living systems.'[20]

From the smallest plant cells up to the Solar System itself, nature is comprised of nested structures and systems, where all exists in relation to all else. We can see the same manifest in work, from the individual up to the organization and beyond to the wider ecosystem of work.

Giles Hutchins writes: 'Over the last 3.8 billion years, nature has survived and flourished through times of radical change and disruption by dynamically networking and collaborating among species and throughout ecosystems. Competition and constraints help shape nature, yet it is collaboration and synergy – not competition – that are responsible for nature's sustained success. The species most able to survive and evolve are those most able to sense and respond, adapt and align, and work in partnership with and within their ecosystems. Diversity, flexibility and collaboration, we find, are core to the interwoven evolutionary journey of life – the driving forces that provide resilience within species and ecosystems...'[10]

In *Aesop's Fables*, we accept that the tortoise and the hare aren't real-life animals actually conversing as they race against each other. Rather, we realize that this is an illustrative tale that reveals insights into contrasting types of human behaviour. In the myths and legends that have been passed down from generation to generation across all cultures, from European to African, the Americas to Australasia, lie lessons about social norms, human nature and the ways we behave as a species.[21]

So, catalysed by the momentous shifts our societies and the planet are going through, we are now discarding the old story of the industrial, mechanistic view of work that has persisted for more than 250 years, and moving into a view more attuned to living systems.

This fresh story of work is both new and ancient. In looking to nature for inspiration for language and metaphors to help us develop a greater understanding of work as a living system, we are nurturing ideas that have been seeded by others.

Humankind has a long history of turning to trees specifically to better understand ourselves and, as Manuel Lima writes in *The Book of Trees*: 'Trees have had such an immense significance to humans there's hardly any culture that hasn't invested them with lofty symbolism and, in many cases, with celestial and religious power.'[22]

It is therefore no surprise that today the natural world continues as a source of storytelling inspiration, even as we increasingly spend more of our time in human-built environments, despite research on the health and wellbeing benefits of spending time in nature.[23] There is even a word for our pull to nature, 'biophilia', coined by Edward O Wilson in 1984 as our 'innate tendency to focus on life and lifelike processes'.[1,24]

In our design of solutions too, humans have long sought to mirror nature, through a practice known as biomimicry[25], such as in the design of aircraft (inspired by birds) or Velcro (inspired by burrs). Within the digital world, design and language have also borrowed from the natural world to help with both familiarity and understanding. Sue Thomas even termed the phrase 'technobiophilia' to capture our tendency to manifest our innate draw to nature within our virtual worlds and online cultures, such as through the use of metaphor as in 'the cloud'.[26]

What's more, there's already a stream of thought that seeks to take inspiration from nature to tell stories that help us better understand the world of work:

- **Gareth Morgan** in *Images of Organization*, in his section on 'Organization as organism' writes: 'most modern organization theorists have looked to nature to understand organizations and organizational life'.[27]
- **Giles Hutchins**, in works such as *The Nature of Business*, dives into nature's principles and laws as inspiration for creating resilient firms of the future.[10]
- **Ken Thompson** draws on the principles of biomimicry to apply nature's lessons to create high-performing teams in *Bioteams*.[28]
- **Arie de Geus**' *The Living Company* is another that explores the concept of the organization as a living organism.[9]

All take the view that in order for organizations to survive, a mindshift is needed to better understand the paradox of chaos and order that exists within organizations and to help us appreciate the many relationships and dependencies within the world of work – through the lens of nature.

At a time when leaders are trying to untangle and re-evaluate behaviours, cultures, purpose and structures within their own organizations, and when humankind, as a whole, is trying to re-establish its relationship with nature, where better to turn for inspiration than nature itself?

And so this is the **Nature of Work**; an understanding of how work and organizations thrive as living systems, interconnected and interdependent, made up of relationships, structures, habitats, biodiversity, and much, much more, inspired by examples we can observe in the natural world. A story that helps us throw off the old story of work, which we've long outgrown as a species, and embrace this new story with courage.

The organization as a forest

The analogy from which we have drawn inspiration to help us create this new language is therefore that of nature. More specifically, in many cases we look to the forest, as a rich example of an intricately interconnected part of nature that contains not only trees, earth, roots, animals, water and plants, but also demonstrates its own life cycle, changing by the season as well as over years and centuries.

A thriving forest exhibits biodiversity, supports a flow of different relationships, shares knowledge, heals and regenerates, can be threatened or destroyed, and has an extensive history and potentially long future if it is allowed to grow and evolve.

In so many different ways, an organization can be compared to a forest, in turn helping that organization to understand its own ecology. By using the forest as a metaphor, leaders and change-makers within an organization can find not only a familiar, relatable story from the natural world but also learn lessons from it. When we observe trees in the forest, at first they appear to be a collection of neighbouring but essentially separate beings – but dig a little deeper and we find that they in fact share resources, growing in a collaborative way that promotes the wellbeing of all trees rather than merely looking after the needs of any single tree.

Beneath the earth, the roots of the forest extend and mingle, and this 'natural infrastructure', while invisible above ground, efficiently relays nutrients, responsively allocating energy and supporting the health of the forest as a whole. Looked at over the course of a year, the forest cycles through the different seasons, with months when new growth is abundant and different parts of the tree flourish, while at other times leaves and branches die back – and organizations can relate their own annual life cycles to these natural patterns of living.

There are animals that live permanently in the forest, others that reside there for a while, and yet more who merely pass through either seasonally or en route to somewhere else – much like a workforce with specific categories of people for different roles, in some sectors varying considerably at particular times of the year. And on the comparisons go.

Nature of Work in 12 elements

To help break down Nature of Work into manageable parts, we have identified 12 elements on which the remainder of this book will focus.

The Nature of Work as a living system is **Purpose**-driven, meaning that work serves not just the organization but also the people within it and the wider society in which it is located. This is because the organization doesn't exist within a vacuum; impacts of decisions it takes ripple across society, while external events likewise ripple back.

An organization's **Roots** ultimately play a key role in how it perceives its purpose, keeping it grounded and stable as external forces whip around. Roots can, however, become unhealthy, meaning new ones may need to be laid down if the organization is to survive.

Strong purpose and roots manifest through the **Habitats** of organizations. This is where work thrives, supported by the physical and virtual habitats in which it takes place. Habitats are inseparable from the people working within those spaces and, without the right habitat, in which people feel they belong and are supported, they can't do their best work.

Those habitats and cultures of belonging can help to nurture **Biodiversity** as an intrinsic element of the living system's health, by creating welcoming environments. Without biodiversity, organizations, and the health of the entire ecosystem of work, stagnate and become at risk.

In **DWG**, we see ourselves as a laboratory for trialling new ways of working. We've grown to a company of 120 people located across Europe and North America, with a fully distributed (work from anywhere) format that has been our lifeblood for more than a decade. Since 2019, we've been experimenting with how a living system, Nature of Work perspective can help us in our thinking.

A recent example was when we hired a new consultant in Europe, who arrived from a global telecoms company. He came from a senior role with a range of skills in the fields of culture, wellness and physical/digital workplace interface, and was intent on a 'portfolio' working week, which would combine his own solo work in these areas alongside digital workplace projects for DWG.

Considering his situation from a **living system** stance, we discussed his options, concluding that, if he were to try and create his own company from scratch, he would be doing so in comparatively 'barren soil'. Instead, he could 'seed' his work within DWG, feeding on the fertile ground of our already mature network, brand, reputation and expert peers, enabling him to grow faster and in a more protected environment.

Using this organic view of the business options allowed us all to see the opportunities for both him and DWG that otherwise might have remained hidden from view.

Seeding new ventures in fertile ground creates the best conditions for growth.

The Nature of Work as a living system is totally dependent on the **Relationships** between that diverse network of people, amongst which knowledge, information and data are exchanged and acted upon.

And while this network may at times seem chaotic, it in fact depends on a multitude of adaptive **Structures**, as people organize themselves and their relationships to help fulfil their shared purpose and bring together their individual strengths.

These people, their relationships and structures all have **Life cycles** that keep the system constantly dynamic and ever-changing, from the length of time someone is with an organization to the longevity of the organization itself.

This natural ebb and flow results in a continual pattern of **Migration**, with a constant stream of people regularly moving between habitats and structures, and sometimes whole organizations on the move too.

Such moves can either be motivated by new opportunities or become inevitable as a result of **Threats** that mean a current habitat is no longer safe. But threats are a critical part of a living system and can help to ensure that organizations stay vigilant to signals of danger, allowing them to respond and adapt in order to keep healthy.

Responses to those threats and opportunities, as well as the intrinsically dynamic nature of life cycles, migration, relationships and other elements, foster a necessary ongoing process of **Regeneration**, unleashing a rolling pattern of fresh life, growth and renewed purpose.

The organization as a living system is ultimately a manifestation of the particular **Intelligence** that emerges out of the collective consciousness of communities. Enabled by an ethics-driven approach to technology, and a deep understanding of what is held as 'sacred', organizations have a unique opportunity to rediscover human intelligence as a part of nature, and technological intelligence as a part of us.

All these elements combine to influence the overall **Health** of the organization. Out of balance, its health will deteriorate, accelerating its life cycle towards death and in turn causing enormous ripple effects on the health of individuals and overall society. Allowed to continually adapt and correct itself to maintain balance between the Nature of Work elements, good health can be sustained, and the living system of work – and all those that belong within it – will be empowered to thrive.

These 12 elements make up the **Nature of Work**, a new story and way of thinking for the living age of work, our place as humans within it, and our relationship with the natural world, for the 2020s and beyond. It is a chance to recognize the threats of the old system and, out of its destruction, to regenerate and grow anew an approach that works for all.

Ask yourself

- What are your immediate feelings and thoughts about drawing inspiration from nature to create a new understanding of work?
- Do any of the 12 Nature of Work elements particularly resonate with you? If so, what is it about that element that intrigues you?
- Have there been times when you've felt as if you've been treated more like a living being than a machine in your working life? What was the impact of this on you?
- Are there parts of your working life that you already think of as a 'living system'? If so, which parts? And what impact does this have?
- Do you think your organization or work community behaves more like a living system or more like a machine at the moment?
- What is your own relationship with the natural world? What beliefs and stories do you have about it?

nature
of work
elements

Our Nature of Work icons (arranged as a natural golden spiral) reveal each element to be a connected part of an overall design leading to the ultimate goal of 'Health'. Change-makers can investigate how each element in their organization relates to the whole.

Illustration by Liad Janes.

Purpose

Roots

Regeneration

Threats

Migration

Intelligence

Health

Life cycles

Structures

Habitats

Biodiversity

Relationships

Purpose

How can you find the deeper purpose of your work and your organization?

Nature: The drive behind different behaviours and elements across the natural world

Work: Why your organization exists

Why are we here?

Over lunch, the CEO of a major software firm confided: 'We are successful on many levels, but do I really know our purpose? We know what we do but not who we are at a deeper level.'

This was at once striking for the honesty but perhaps a little alarming that we work in a world where we can 'succeed' without ever truly knowing our purpose. It is refreshing (but maybe surprisingly not that uncommon) to see such self-awareness revealed quietly at the C-level in many organizations. It reflects the limitations of our shared historical and habitual mechanistic mindsets and cultures.

A machine can execute on its remit without ever needing to have any deeper purpose than the production of service X or product Y. But when we experience that with (in the case of this CEO) more than 60,000 human beings on staff worldwide, we feel the revealed emptiness at the heart of work.

A new breed of organization is emerging against this backdrop, which not only has a sense of its purpose of survival (for example, making a profit) but also a deeper understanding of its interconnected purpose and the role it plays in bettering our world.

Nature as purpose-driven

So, what is the purpose of the tree above you? The soil beneath your feet? The worker ant that forages? The plant that turns towards the sunlight? The polar bear cubs that play fight each other (*see p.33*) – or any of the myriad other behaviours we can observe around us every day in the natural world? They are all purpose-driven. They all have an interconnected sense of purpose.

These behaviours have all evolved to allow the various species to feed, find shelter, reproduce, build relationships and survive. And yet, these 'purposes' are always interconnected in nature, serving both the survival of the organism itself while also contributing to the resilience of the overall ecosystem.

Trees, for instance, absorb carbon dioxide and breathe out oxygen – that crucial element

The **Purpose Power Index** aims to measure what consumers think about a brand's purpose, with 'purpose' understood as the brand's mission in society: 'the higher order reason to exist beyond making profit'. In compiling the Index, brands are assessed on whether they have a higher purpose in society other than just making money, such as: improving the lives of people and their communities; being committed to changing the world for the better; and taking actions that not only benefit shareholders, employees or customers but society as a whole. A 2019 survey found that a 'new kind of brand leader has arrived', naming brands such as **Etsy**, **Ben & Jerry's**, **Toms** and **Burt's Bees**, which are not only recognized by consumers as being purpose-driven, but also perform well financially.[29] The rise of social and environmental B corporations is another example of this movement.

Oriental pied hornbill, Singapore. Fruits are part of the interconnected purpose of natural systems, protecting seeds, allowing plant regeneration and supplying nutrients to other species. Clear purpose in work brings a diverse range of benefits to stakeholders.

needed by all life on Earth. They also help to combat soil erosion and run-off by absorbing water through their roots (*see opposite*). These roots quite evidently exist on one level to feed and structurally support the individual tree, but it is perhaps less obvious that they also have multiple other functions, such as connecting that tree with its neighbours, assisting in a cooperative way with the distribution of resources, relaying signals, and so much more.

In another example of the interconnected purpose of natural systems, fruit initially provides protection for the valuable seeds contained within its usually fleshy outer, then later enables the diffusion of those seeds so that the species can continue in the next generation.[30] In parallel with this, any animals that feed on those fruits and seeds will benefit from crucial nutrients to support their own survival.

The creatures and plants that we see across nature are at any one time fulfilling multiple purposes: contributing to the overall health of the ecosystem, while also striving to survive themselves. It is impossible to uncouple one from the other; both the full living system of nature and the individual within it rely on one another to contribute to and fulfil their purpose.

What does purpose mean to you?

This interconnected sense of purpose that we observe in nature can also help us to understand our own personal sense of purpose, and how that in turn relates to the purpose of organizations as living systems.

'Purpose' for humans is a multi-layered and crucial concept, meaning different things to different people, across cultures and depending on the context.

In Japan, the notion of *ikigai* is often translated as 'that which makes life worth living'. *Ikigai* encompasses both large themes, such as work and family life, as well as seemingly 'smaller' but nevertheless impactful activities, such as hobbies and travel.[31] It balances both interconnected purpose (the self in community) and individual interest (the self alone).

For the Shona people of Mozambique and Zimbabwe, the purpose of life is traditionally believed to be 'to love' in order to make the world a better place in which to live. 'Love' here is understood as the basis of all relationships, inspiring respect for human dignity and forming the backbone of communal life.[32]

At a psychological level, purpose has likewise been found to result from achieving a balance between the self and community: 'a stable and generalized intention to accomplish something that is at once meaningful to the self and of consequence to the world beyond the self'.[33] In other words, our individual sense of purpose isn't just related to meeting our own desires and needs but also to the role we play in contributing to our larger communal circles.

If we are able to discern purpose within our organizations as serving this broader urge that humans have to both give and receive, we can begin to understand how organizational purpose is deeply interconnected with wider society.

Florin Rotar, **Avanade**'s Modern Workplace Global Lead, works with some of the world's largest organizations and sees a link between purpose, engagement and company performance: 'Work seems to be becoming more focused on meaningful purpose, such as human impact, societal impact, sustainability, diversity and inclusion, in addition to the usual goals such as shareholder value. If you use the analogy of nature, a tree has a deeper purpose, which is to live. Organizations that have a deeper and more meaningful purpose that goes beyond shareholder value tend to be more successful because they engage with their people on a deeper level. This is also going to be more important for new generations.'[34]

Gallup's 2019 Employee Engagement survey found that 35% of US workers were 'engaged', a record high since Gallup started tracking engagement in 2000. However, 52% of respondents still fell into the 'not engaged' category, with 13% 'actively disengaged'.[35] An engaged worker has been defined by Gallup as one who is highly involved in, enthusiastic about and committed to work and their workplace. It's been found to be determined by factors such as how clear you feel about your role, having the chance to do what you do best, opportunities to develop strong co-worker relationships, and working with a common mission or purpose.

This impressive network of roots not only supplies the tree with essential nutrients but has a wider purpose of protecting its local environment against damaging soil erosion.

Schoolchildren protest on environmental issues in 2019. Attitude surveys show that this generation expects (even demands) advanced environmental practice from companies or they will refuse to work for or even buy from such organizations.

Elizabeth Lotardo, Vice President of Client Services at a management consulting firm, writes: 'We have an inherent desire to be part of something that's bigger than ourselves... Organizations are seeing the economic benefits and people are seeing the personal benefits... Collectively, the world is moving toward a **sense of purpose**.'[36]

The well-established organic food company **Riverford** delivers fruit, vegetables and an increasing range of other locally grown and produced food goods across the UK. With **ethical and ecological practices** at the core of the business, it has also recently introduced a high degree of employee ownership; 74% of the company is owned by an Employee Trust, an approach that's deliberately been chosen to 'protect it from predators' that might be looking to buy it, as well as to uphold its core values. These comprise: 'Giving a fair deal to staff, suppliers, customers and the planet; a commitment to organic and to our farming roots; long-term relationships of trust with our growers.'[37]

Future generations seek purpose in work

Each new generation that enters the world of work brings with it a different perspective on purpose. And, even within that generation, these needs and views will evolve as the people of that generation move through their own **Life cycles**: priorities change as people grow older, regardless of which named generation they are identified with.

Much has been written about Generation Y, also known as Millennials (and not all of it fair). But among this generation – those born from about 1980 to the mid-1990s – we can discern a pattern around their quest for purpose through work. There is a common desire to actively seek out and forge a meaningful work/life balance, with flexibility, creativity and encouragement from work as explicit goals – and with the achievement of these aims increasingly enabled by more mature digital workplaces.

For Generation Z, which roughly spans the mid-1990s to 2010s, it has been found that cultures of inclusion are essential, with this cohort particularly valuing **Biodiversity** and drawn to organizations that are demonstrably good 'global citizens' and actively committed to addressing societal challenges.[38]

Then after Generation Z comes Generation Alpha, the global community of schoolchildren, large numbers of whom have already shown a willingness to protest and strike, highlighting and standing up for what they see as essential for the future of the planet. The mission of many of these young people is to set the stage for what they believe to be the most profound – and increasingly urgent – purpose of humanity: addressing the societal and environmental challenges and crises we face, so that the world they will inherit is sustainable.

It is anticipated that this dedication to values is something they will bring with them as they move into the world of work, ready to criticize and reject organizations they perceive to be part of the problem rather than working towards solutions.[39] And while it's not yet known how the experience of being a child during a global health crisis will impact their future careers and aims in work, early indications suggest it has prompted some to consider working in medicine, science and education.[40] Meanwhile, other young people are already finding purpose in helping those who have been badly affected by the pandemic, for example by raising funds to provide meals for those in food poverty, teaching online classes to younger children, or writing to seniors in retirement communities.[41]

This is a seismic transformation in what might be demanded or expected of employers from their prospective new employee intake – and it will challenge many organizations in ways for which they are largely unprepared. It will require companies to truly identify what it is that keeps them rooted and connected to their surrounding environment.

Started in 2012, the company **Who Gives A Crap** manufactures and sells toilet paper, paper towels and tissues. It was founded with the specific purpose of generating funds that would be used to help build toilets and improve sanitation in developing countries, while also ensuring that all its products are made from **environmentally sustainable resources** and its work practices are ethical.[42]

Xylem, a company offering a variety of 'wastewater and water solutions', positions much of its activity around sustainability and has a motto 'Let's solve water'. This alludes not only to its products and services, but also to broader environmental, health and humanitarian solutions. Much of its purpose-driven work is carried out through a comprehensive CSR programme called **Watermark**. This aims to 'provide education and access to safe water to ensure healthy lives, gender equality and resilient communities'.[43]

Does your organization have deep purpose?

Historically, an organization would define its purpose as being 'what it does'. This could be, for example, manufacturing, retail, hospitality. While this has helped many succeed, this rather simplistic understanding of 'purpose' is born out of a mechanistic mindset.

What we can learn from purpose in nature, as well as from what we as humans need as purpose, is that people in organizations can develop a more interconnected understanding of why their organization exists by considering the impact it has – and can have – on society.

We are already in an era of what we would call 'deep purpose', where a sense of societal value and contribution is beginning to flow through organizations. Without that deep purpose, future generations will not consider working for you, with you, or even having any interaction as consumers with the company. Already, in the here and now, decisions are being made by employees and consumers about the organizations with which they wish to be associated.

More and more, organizations and companies are being called on by their employees, customers and society to adopt a stance and take meaningful action within areas that impact the wider ecosystem of society:

Actions of organizations have ripple effects not only on their employees and their families but also on society and the local and wider environment.

the environment, issues of race and gender inequality, accessibility and social mobility.

Organizations whose working practices and business models harm their people are coming under the spotlight too, particularly in warehouse and factory environments, but also in terms of zero-hours contracts and within the 'gig economy'.

Unintended, as well as unforeseen, consequences of products and services are increasingly being considered, particularly within the technology sector, resulting in movements like Tech for Good, which focuses on promoting more ethically conscious practices.[44]

What's more, people are attuned to identifying, and prepared to call out, those who are 'performing' for a marketing initiative rather than truly embedding environmental and social impact values deep within their purpose. This has led to accusations of 'greenwashing' (environmental) or 'pinkwashing' (LGBTQIA+) becoming increasingly common.[45] Organizations that were quick to publish vague, box-ticking statements in support of the Black Lives Matter movement were criticized over a lack of Black people on their boards, within their workforces, or in some cases for having a history of practices harmful to Black communities.[14]

An approach that doesn't bring deep purpose into the heart of your organization will ultimately harm its **Health**, not just in the long term but increasingly in the immediate term too.

Finding your organization's interconnected purpose

Decisions and practices adopted within an organization will have ripple effects, not just on the lives of its people and their families, but also on the wider society in which that organization resides.

As strategic designer Cassie Robinson suggests in a blog post entitled *Beyond human-centred design, to?*, there is a deep need to bring these ripples closer in to the way services and products are designed within organizations, including for employees. This will help them more empathetically consider their impact on families, communities, society and the planet.[46] In the 'old world' language of the organization, conceived during the industrial age, 'purpose' is easily and narrowly defined. As Peter Senge writes: 'A machine exists for a purpose conceived of by its builders. Again, this is the conventional view of a company: its purpose is to make as much money as possible for its owners.'[9]

In our 'new world' language of the living age, the purpose of the organization is both to thrive internally, by helping its people find purpose, but also to contribute positively to the vitality of its wider ecosystem by finding and fulfilling its own purpose within society.

This purpose-driven approach to work was put under the spotlight as never before due to COVID-19. The contribution of organizations – or lack of it – to resolving the many urgent and widespread problems and needs thrown up by the pandemic became seen as signals of just how healthy and trustworthy those organizations were. Indeed, many organizations are finding renewed purpose in the face of the multitude of challenges now confronting us as a species.

The Edelman Trust Barometer, in particular, found that organizations which put their profits before supporting and protecting their own people contributed to a decrease in trust in those businesses. Other factors that impacted trust included to what extent businesses were working to protect their smaller suppliers.[13] The outcome was clear: organizations should be looking out for their people and the bigger

Unilever has a high-level **Sustainable Living Plan**, comprising a strategy and roadmap with objectives that dictate multiple sub-strategies and initiatives, right down to the branding of different products.[47] In 2018, 28 'Sustainable Living' brands owned by Unilever, which are positioned as 'taking action to support positive change for people and the planet', grew 69% faster than the rest of Unilever's business.[48]

Two young polar bear cubs play on pack ice, Arctic Ocean, north of Svalbard. Play fighting supports the young bears' purpose, which at this point in their life cycle is to learn skills to equip them for surviving in their challenging habitat. In the workplace, alternative approaches to learning draw on latent energy to enhance skills.

US tech company **Bloom Energy** usually makes green-energy fuel cells but during the COVID-19 pandemic found a way to fix and repurpose broken ventilators that had originally been stockpiled to deal with bird flu in the mid-noughties and had been sitting unused ever since. They initially delivered a batch of 170 to treat those with severe COVID-19 symptoms.[49]

Meanwhile, some larger firms, such as **Estee Lauder Companies**, made significant donations to help combat the impact of the pandemic and also used existing production facilities to manufacture supplies of hand sanitizer, which were donated to high-need groups and frontline staff.[50]

ecosystem in the present crisis, rather than focusing solely on profits.[13] What's more, stories of organizations who were able to repurpose themselves to contribute to solving the complex challenges thrown up by the pandemic have been lauded.[51]

Just imagine what your organization could be

By thinking of an organization as a living system, not just within itself but also as a single organism that is part of a larger ecosystem, this transformational change in purpose can seem more possible and less challenging. What is your organization's role within that larger ecosystem? What are its strengths that can be put to the wider good of society?

Imagine your organization, but with social responsibility at its heart and core rather than just around the edges, or as an afterthought or add-on. That is the shift which is coming.

Legitimacy to exist as a company or public organization will flow from how clearly you are able to find its deeper purpose within society. Elements that have historically been considered nice-to-have 'extras' – sustainability, social contribution, community engagement – will become the pulse of your work. Without that, not only will future generations simply ignore your organization, but even sooner than that, its **Health** and sustainability will start to tilt out of balance and die.

Many organizations are already on this path to finding their purpose – but without the intensity and full-blown commitment required. The question of finding deep purpose may present the greatest threat for many organizations.

The opportunities here are far-reaching for those who embrace the shift and who are able to adapt and evolve with the changing elements and threats that surround them.

Ask yourself

- What is your personal purpose as an individual in work? How has that purpose driven the decisions you've made throughout your career? And has it changed over time?

- What values matter to you and how do you act on them in your work life? Do they align with those of your organization or work community? If not, what can you do about it?

- How do people in your organization or work community define their collective purpose at the moment? Who does that purpose serve?

- What is or could be, the deeper, interconnected purpose of your organization

or work community, so that it can fulfil its own needs and the needs of society?

- How might that deeper purpose enhance the health of your organization or work community in time?

- What current habits, patterns and practices would finding that deeper purpose challenge?

- Do you truly believe your organization's purpose can evolve? Do others believe that too?

Roots

What are the unseen foundations and systems that underpin your organization?

Nature: The part of a plant that grows into the ground to hold it steady and also brings it nourishment from its surrounding environment

Work: The hidden systems, structures and stories that underpin an organization

Connected roots

For some reason, the energy industry has always had a strong sense of its roots. Maybe it's because it needs to plan forward for a decade or more, or due to the scale of each project, but this is a sector that has long put a premium on sharing knowledge well and adapting over time.

At **GE**, forums for sharing learnings and insights, as well as enabling questions to be resolved by peers, have been around for some 20 years, stretching back to the early days of the modern internet.[52] It has long been essential that anyone joining the company as a new hire becomes deeply engaged with the culture and practice of sharing knowledge; this is foundational to working there. The technical systems that facilitate knowledge transfer and 'post-action reviews', as well as the process and culture of sharing knowledge, have always been part of the 'root systems' of the company – and, in fact, this is general across the entire industry too.

Such 'roots' extend beneath the surface of organizations and are so much a part of their way of working that they lie almost hidden from view – and yet play a crucial role in laying the foundations for the rest of work.

Looking forward, as the **Purpose** of the energy industry is under greater scrutiny than ever before due to its huge environmental impact, taking that strong heritage of knowledge and applying it to more renewable forms of energy will be crucial. The roots of many companies in the energy sector stretch back over a hundred years, infused with history and memory, even as new companies have emerged. Will those roots help them connect with a deeper, more interconnected purpose in the present and into the future?

At **Proctor and Gamble**'s global headquarters in Cincinatti, Ohio, all new North American employees get a tour of the Archives Center. **Greg McCoy**, Senior Archivist, comments: 'Our staff take employees and their guests on a 179-year journey using the themes of passion, serendipity and challenging paradigms to bring our heritage to life while making it relevant and applicable to their backgrounds and interest level. We also work closely with HR to ensure all new North American interns and employees experience the tour and are aware of the historical relevance of P&G's purpose, values and principles.'[53]

Methuselah tree, a 4,853-year-old Great Basin bristlecone pine, Inyo National Forest, California – considered to be the oldest tree in the world. Every organization has its founders and origin stories, acting as reference points to inform the present.

Paul remembers a story from his own family: 'My father as a young man sold furniture fabrics. On a trip to the English county of Yorkshire in the late 1960s, he met two enthusiastic young entrepreneurs who asked him for credit to get their new furniture business off the ground. He helped them out and now in the UK the **DFS** sofa brand is huge – a successful company with 5,000 employees and annual revenue of around £1 billion.' The roots of DFS matter and inform the **company culture** to this day, remaining at the heart a 'family company'.[54]

Levi Strauss & Co official archivist **Tracey Panek** preserves historical garments, designs and records, which she says helps to 'assist employees to understand the brand's evolution'.[55]

The hidden heritage and knowledge of forests

We can't be sure of the oldest tree in the world but it is believed to be Methuselah, a 4,853-year-old Great Basin bristlecone pine (*see opposite*) in the White Mountains of California[56], named after the supposed oldest man to ever live (to the ripe old age of 969 as told in the Bible).

Of course, while an individual tree can grow over many centuries, the forest where it resides is also ever evolving, and the most ancient forest in the world, stretching back to prehistoric times, is 100–180 million years old. The Daintree Rainforest, close to the Great Barrier Reef, is the largest rainforest on the Australian continent, with more than 12,000 species of insect and 3,000 plant varieties (*see pp.39–40*).[57] When we see this forest, we are looking at a landscape that dinosaurs would also have witnessed.

Ecologists have discovered that the roots of the aspen tree can date back thousands of years, meaning that if you see one before you, it's likely connected through its roots back to an ancient history, intelligence and wisdom to the memory of its surrounding forest.

Far from being a discrete aspen tree standing in front of you, its roots beneath the ground will stretch out into a shared network, connecting that tree's roots with those of its neighbours. Each aspen tree is in effect a 'branch' growing from one root. While individual trees may die, the roots carry on and new shoots grow, creating aspen colonies joined by a single root system and with a life span way beyond that of each tree. Indeed, the huge aspen colony of 40,000 trees in central Utah, nicknamed 'Pando'

('I spread' in Latin), is thought to be 80,000 years old, and is often described as a single organism, despite looking to us like a forest.[58]

This root network that nurtures all forests has become known colloquially as the 'wood wide web'. A complex underground ecosystem of lace-like fungus reaches out within the soil, connecting different trees via their roots (*see p.45*). This network exists in part as a mutual exchange of nutrients between fungus and tree. But much, much more than that, it serves to support the entire forest.[59]

Through these ancient roots, an **Intelligence** is shared. For example, a dying tree will deliberately extract fewer resources from the soil so that others can receive more. Warnings are sent out via the root systems from trees that find themselves under attack to alert others so that they can prepare to defend themselves.[60] There is a constant flow of information being communicated between individual trees, which helps the forest to survive as a community.

Moreover, the roots of a tree, as well as delivering essential nutrients to it from the soil and connecting it with its neighbours, also serve to anchor and stabilize it. Above ground, trees are exposed to all the elements – the whipping wind, rainstorms, flooding, the heat of the Sun, the weight of snow and ice. The tree's roots are essential to withstand the movement these forces can cause and in securing it to the earth, while simultaneously also supporting the earth itself against **Threats** such as landslides. The roots start out fine in form as they grip around soil elements to spur on the early shoots, then become larger and sturdier as the tree ages and expands outwards and upwards.

This hidden, vast network of roots that thrives beneath the surface is foundational to how both individual trees and fully connected forests are able to survive. They've evolved to enable growth and communication, and to provide stability and collaboration.

The shared roots of trees have a deep interconnected **Purpose**: they serve as both the knowledge 'network' between individual trees, and signify the long history and life span of the interconnected forest. Within them lies both heritage and '**Intelligence**', all hidden from the view of those above ground.

Finding heritage in your roots

The roots of an organization, those very first elements of growth that are often unseen and yet continue to keep it grounded, are essential in informing it and others of 'who' the organization is. They help to tell its origin story, describe the environment in which it was first 'seeded' and explain how it has changed and evolved over time. These roots ultimately help to anchor that organization in the past, present and future.

Some organizations have roots that stretch back hundreds of years, laid down in a time that was very different to the world in which we currently find ourselves. Within their present cultures and stories will no doubt lie practices and knowledge that have evolved out of what came before. Some of these will be retained and some cast off, for better or for worse. Other organizations have new roots that are still fresh, only recently developed, which need to be protected and nurtured if they are to be allowed to flourish over time.

As we shall see in **Life cycles**, there is evidence that the life span of organizations has been decreasing over recent years. For those seeking to survive, combining a renewed understanding of their interconnected **Purpose** with a deep understanding of their roots, and being able to align the two, is essential. That reconciliation of who an organization and its people were at its start with who it is today – and will be in the future – requires a level of adaptability and honesty, allowing it to delve into those roots and what they mean for the organization, its people and wider society today.

When organizations lose sight and clarity, or get diverted from their core purpose, leaders (either sensibly or in a panic) may advocate that: 'We need to get back to our roots.' To do this successfully, work is required to recognize what those roots actually are.

As such, many organizations place considerable value on researching, documenting and exhibiting their heritage, with some going as far as to employ an official company historian or archivist. For many organizations, this can prove a real bonus; the origin, roots and heritage of an organization become established as part of the brand story and mystique, attracting both customers and employees.

For others, digging deeper into the organization's hidden history can reveal some uncomfortable truths. However, if recognized and dealt with proactively, even these less favourable revelations can be helpfully addressed as part of a reconciliation and **Regeneration** process, serving to identify and consolidate a renewed **Purpose**.

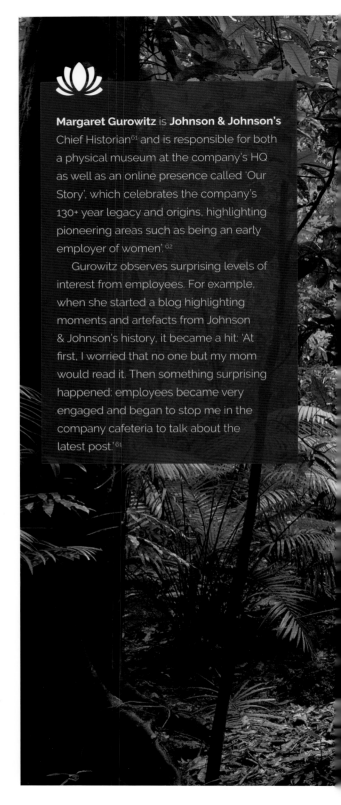

Margaret Gurowitz is **Johnson & Johnson's** Chief Historian[61] and is responsible for both a physical museum at the company's HQ as well as an online presence called 'Our Story', which celebrates the company's 130+ year legacy and origins, highlighting pioneering areas such as being an early employer of women'.[62]

Gurowitz observes surprising levels of interest from employees. For example, when she started a blog highlighting moments and artefacts from Johnson & Johnson's history, it became a hit: 'At first, I worried that no one but my mom would read it. Then something surprising happened: employees became very engaged and began to stop me in the company cafeteria to talk about the latest post.'[63]

Mossman Gorge, Daintree National Park, Queensland, Australia: the oldest forest in the world. The roots of any organization are alive, usually unseen in the present and yet connected to its history.

English Heritage, an organization that looks after more than 400 historic sites and buildings across England, commissioned research in 2007 into which buildings under its stewardship had roots and connections in the slave trade.[63] The organization has been working ever since to incorporate its findings on the colonial heritage of its various buildings into the visitor experience, as well as adding this history to related guidebooks and online content. Much has been achieved on this front but English Heritage accepts there is still more work to do in bringing this too often untold side of history fully into the open.[64] Acknowledging the hard truths that may lie buried in an organization's historical roots can actually help its people to find the drive for its purpose today.

Quaking aspens, Vail, Colorado, US: aspens have one common root system. The energy and value in a company might appear to come from distinct divisions or brands, but underneath the surface, resources and dynamism are often shared.

When **Oxfam International** embarked on a global digital workplace programme, which involved introducing Workplace from Facebook, Box and other systems, this was designed to help **knowledge sharing and collaboration** across a global network of different and diverse entities and employees, often working in remote areas. The programme has resulted in a shift in Oxfam's culture, giving employees the confidence to reach out to colleagues from across the world to ask questions, seek advice from experts and make connections.[65]

The first wave of the pandemic saw thousands of staff in the UK's **National Health Service** (**NHS**) redeployed from their normal duties in non-urgent medical areas to roles that would support the fight against COVID-19 and allow hospitals to maintain emergency services. For example, the **North Tees and Hartlepool NHS Trust** moved nurses, healthcare assistants and even physiotherapists over to new services. One team, the Oxygen Runners at University Hospital in North Tees, monitored the use of oxygen throughout the hospital to support clinical staff on the frontline; the team included podiatrists, audiologists, occupational therapists, speech therapists, radiographers, nurses, and more.[66]

Origins and roots often exert more influence than is acknowledged. They can be a significant factor in attracting employees to work for a company in the first place and then helping to keep them engaged once employed. Roots can also play a part in shaping strategies and influencing the actions of leaders who want to build on what has been before, helping to drive organizational **Purpose** and value.

On the other hand, it can be attractive to others when an organization does not yet have deep roots. This can make working for a startup an appealing option, or even act as a driver to launch a new business. Both scenarios bring the opportunity to be involved in creating the heritage of the company for the future, without the need to balance this with the legacy of 'who' it was in the past.

Just as in the forest, where individual trees die while the root system carries on, an organization's heritage is an integral part of its story, even as people and **Structures** come and go. For some, that historical root system is well-known; for others, it remains hidden. For those seeking renewed **Purpose** for the living age, knowing – and reconciling – an organization's heritage can provide an important starting point.

Knowledge flows through shared roots

This story of 'roots' as an organization's heritage is also deeply interlinked with how knowledge and memory flow from past to present, from present to future, and between individuals, teams and whole organizations.

As we saw earlier, roots serve to both 'ground' trees to the earth and sustain forests over time, while also connecting individual trees into a large superorganism that can share information and efficiently allocate resources. Thinking about this natural system can help us to visualize the similarly intricate web of communication and collaboration through which resources, knowledge, memory and information flow within and between organizations. Just as the trees have their own 'wood wide web' (*see pp.43–44*), so too do people, teams and organizations.

Far too often, the elaborate, invisible network through which people in and across organizations are connected is underdeveloped, patchy or even broken. This has the effect of isolating people from both one another day to day as well as from 'who' the organization is at its roots and in its **Purpose**. Likewise, it is all too common to see organizations fracture into silos or become mired in internal politics, preventing teams of people from working together as a unified living system with shared roots.

Individuals may well be able to be self-sufficient for a period, drawing resources from their immediate environment. However, ultimately, this will not allow them to thrive in as effective a way as if they were connected with others across the organization. Moreover, if they need help, they can't reach out. And if individuals aren't thriving, the overall **Health** of the organization suffers as a result.

Taking a living system view of the organization provides a broader perspective that, in time, can transform energy wasted on harmful competition and power struggles into collective focus.

How can we make sure that people are properly connected through this foundational 'root system', meaning they can successfully communicate, collaborate and share resources and knowledge with each other, while also being connected into the heritage and **Purpose** of the organization? How can you and people in your organization or work community help to nurture the existence and effectiveness of that communication network?

It is here that elements of the digital workplace, such as collaboration tools and knowledge management and learning programmes, emerge as critical in helping us to connect with one other.

Such initiatives are deeply rooted in enabling people to connect around shared **Purpose**, facilitating effective communication and 'unlocking' the flow of knowledge around an organization. These technological and cultural networks that combine people are essential for helping work to happen, even more so during – and presumably after – the global COVID-19 pandemic, where fewer people than ever are co-located in shared physical **Habitats**.

Combined with shared **Purpose**, this deep network of roots, which allows people to connect with one another and share knowledge and stories, can form the foundational system through which an organization's work community is created and sustained over time.

Conceptualizing an organization's root system is therefore an essential way of understanding how the people within its community today connect with those who came before them, with one another in the present, and with those who will come after them. Through this root

system, memory, knowledge, communication and learning can all flow through both time and space.

Diverting resources through the root system

There is, however, one final lesson to be learned from the way in which trees in a forest are connected via their roots. We saw how forests have evolved to be able to divert resources as needed, based on the health of individual trees.

How can we better discern when and how to divert essential resources to different parts of the organization, and indeed society, according to emergent need? For example, when the need or appetite for a particular sector of an organization's products or services is declining, then reducing resources and effort devoted to that area could allow the energy to be harnessed elsewhere.

Are we able to consider who – and what – outside of the organization *isn't* a part of its current root system and so is excluded from communication, knowledge flows and resource sharing? This might appear to include customers, supply chains, alumni, future generations of workers and families of current workers – but it could also include the natural environment, or other societal systems and institutions. All these are already within the organization's ecosystem – but are they a part of its communication and knowledge web? To what extent are people aware of the resources they are extracting for themselves that may be needed for others?

Beneath every forest and wood there is a complex underground web of roots, fungi and bacteria helping to connect trees and plants to one another. This subterranean 'social' network, up to 500 million years old, has become known as the 'wood wide web'. *Illustration © Macrina Busato*

Healthy fast-food chain **Leon UK** redirected resources to support health workers in the NHS during the COVID-19 pandemic. Working with others, it launched **FeedNHS**, creating a network of restaurants, suppliers and delivery services, which helped to deliver and fund free meals to NHS staff during the peak of the health crisis. This coalition was able to work together as a united, living system and 'by sharing contacts and learnings daily on an 11am conference call, helped each other to reach 102 hospitals in total... serving over 1.5 million meals'.[67]

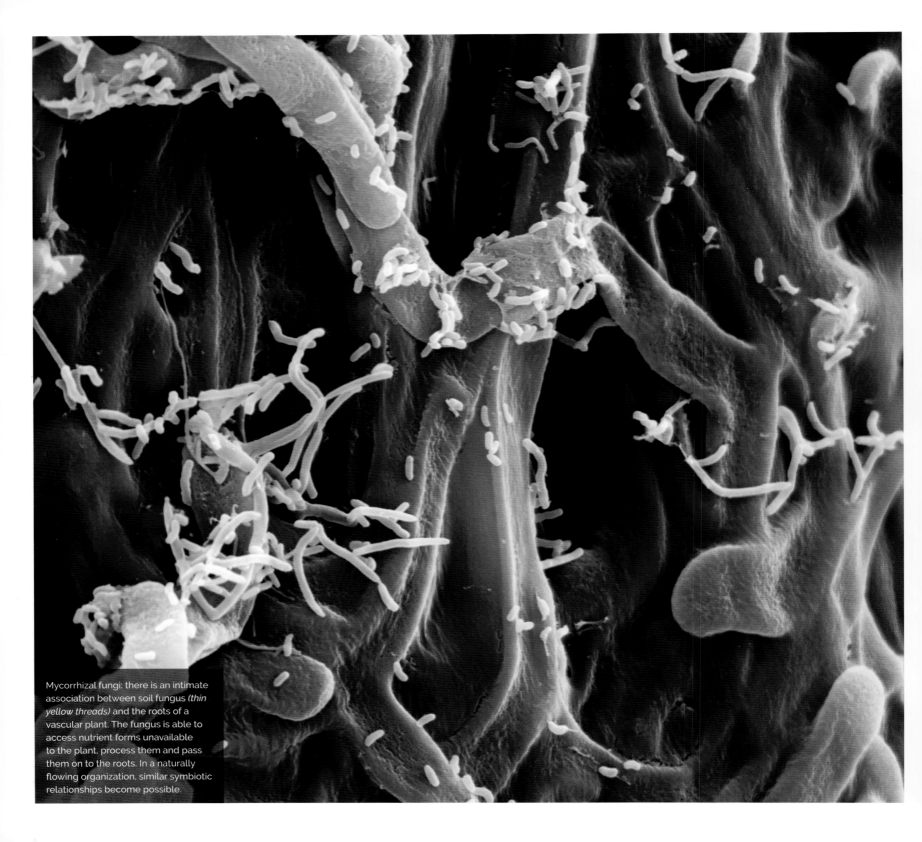

Mycorrhizal fungi: there is an intimate association between soil fungus *(thin yellow threads)* and the roots of a vascular plant. The fungus is able to access nutrient forms unavailable to the plant, process them and pass them on to the roots. In a naturally flowing organization, similar symbiotic relationships become possible.

The response to the COVID-19 pandemic showed how people within organizations were quickly able to realize and act upon the fact that we're all ultimately connected through one 'root system' and part of the same 'forest'. They were able to rapidly share resources, improve communication and enhance collaboration, whether that be between people within the organization or through creating new connections into broader society.

As the **Purpose** of different organizations becomes more interconnected, their root systems will likewise expand as more people and elements become included in who is considered to be part of their 'forest', enabling both greater knowledge sharing and richer understanding of the heritage of the organization.

In an organization's roots, its past, present and future all live, simultaneously. All it takes is the courage to become deeply acquainted with those roots, and to help them inform what comes next for the organization.

Ask yourself

- What do you consider your own roots and heritage to be? How has that informed your choices over the course of your career, and how might it inform them in the future?

- How aware are people in your organization or work community of its origins and foundational roots? What stories have been passed down about its heritage, and which stories are left untold?

- Does that heritage still influence your organization's purpose and, if so, how?

- Does your organization's recognized heritage enable people today, or does it hinder growth and stability? If the latter, how can people evolve what the organization's history says about its purpose?

- To what extent do people in your organization or work community today feel connected to those who came before them and to those who will come after them?

- Do people in your organization or work community behave as isolated single trees? Or do they behave more like a forest, with a connected root system through which they support each other?

- How well are people connected with each other through your organization's digital workplace? Does knowledge and communication flow easily between people? If not, what could be preventing those connections?

- Does the root system stop at the boundaries of your organization or work community? If so, how can this be extended to better connect its people with external people and institutions, to increase the flow of knowledge, communication and resources for all?

Habitats

What are the physical, digital and natural workplaces in which you work best?

Nature: The natural environment in which an organism lives

Work: The physical and digital workplaces where work thrives

Work has left the building

During the 2010s, **DWG** would often facilitate sessions on creating 'human-centred digital workplaces worth working in'. We'd typically feature examples, stories and insights into how work was becoming a portable, mobile experience – something you do, rather than somewhere you go. In the following Q&A session, you could be sure to hear variants of the following reactions:

- 'In our company, we're allowed to work remotely in theory, but how can we do that when managers expect us in the office?'
- 'Isn't it hard to force yourself to work when you are at home?'
- 'How do you know anyone is doing their work when you can't see them?'
- 'This will never happen in our company.'
- 'How do you build trust when you aren't together in person?'

Then 2020 arrived and half the workforce globally left the office, likely to return only partially, seldom – or never. Not only did the world of work keep on turning but people were generally more productive and often hugely surprised that it actually worked so well. And this was despite the many extra challenges people were facing related to working from home during a pandemic, such as digital fatigue, lack of in-person social connection, and having to share space with family members and housemates.[68] Almost all large organizations (including those like **Google**, which had previously been firmly committed to in-person working) decided that this flexible, distributed way of working could become the standard, not just for 2020 but forever. You decide where to work – and when.

In July 2020, **Roland Busch**, Deputy CEO of German-headquartered engineering firm **Siemens**, announced that the company's 'New Normal Working Model' would take its working policy 'a step further' on the back of COVID-19, allowing 140,000 staff in 125 locations to work remotely two or three days a week if they wish to – permanently. Busch explained: 'The basis for this forward-looking working model is further development of our corporate culture. These changes will also be associated with a different leadership style, one that focuses on outcomes rather than on time spent at the office.'[69]

White polar fox, perfectly adapted to its Arctic habitat, Svalbard, Norway.

It turns out all the scepticism of the post-talk Q&A was based on an illusion. The problems cited never really existed; they were just habitual practices and routines that could be broken and reimagined, as it happened, virtually overnight. Once we experience a habitat that suits us, we want to make that environment, that place, into our home.

In the case of work, that 'place' is both physical and virtual, partly where we are each day or moment physically, but also where we are digitally. Modern work habitats are places we select in real time that allow us to work where and as we wish.

This 2020 transformation, when more than 40% of the modern workforce left the office never to return (according to industry research group Gartner[70]), serves as an extraordinary large-scale exemplar of what can happen when an organization experiences itself as a living system, dynamically responding to both the human needs of its people and of wider society.

The nature of habitats

When April arrives in the English Cotswolds, where Paul lives, the garden, fields and woods that surround his home are perfectly adapted for all manner of wildlife. There are particular areas of grasses and undergrowth that are attractive to the rabbits and hares; the robins return to their ideal nesting spots, selected and refined in previous years; and the field mice scurry around near the dry stone walls where they know they will feel safe and protected. Clearly, they are all in their ideal habitat. They feel at ease, at home, secure.

An organism's natural habitat is simply the environment to which it has adapted to best survive. Its needs are met – it has access to food, shelter, water; it is where it can thrive, as long as the habitat itself remains healthy.

Earth has evolved a vast range of different habitats, from forests to deserts to the marine habitats of the open seas. Each has its own ecosystem and features that have helped specific animals and plants to adapt. The Arctic fox, with its thick, white fur, is perfectly adapted to its habitat in the Arctic regions (*see pp.47–48*), while the Bengal fox is better suited to the open, short grasslands of the Indian sub-continent.

And as habitats transform with the changing seasons, the behaviours of those that live within them likewise shift; we see some animals hibernating for winter as temperatures drop, having made sure first to stock up on food during autumn. Others migrate to warmer climes, travelling far and wide. Spring brings with it new life and summer adds the heat of the Sun to ripen food sources – and so the cycle goes on.

Habitats and those who live within them are so closely intertwined within the living system of nature as to be inseparable. And it is when natural habitats come under **Threat** and change rapidly – as so many of the forests and other environments on Earth currently are – that those who call them home likewise come under threat, forced to permanently **Migrate** to new habitats or risk their very survival.

Craving habitats where we feel alive

Don't we all – both at home and at work – crave that knowledge and feeling that we are in our right place? The Danes and Norwegians, for example, have a word, *hygge*, which is defined as that sensation of enjoying 'coziness' and comfortable conviviality with a warm inner glow of wellness and contentment.[71]

Estimates indicate that people spend at least 90% of time within human-built environments.[72] What habitats are we creating for ourselves when we work? Are they designed for us to thrive? How do the spaces we occupy affect our behaviour, our wellness, how we think and feel?

And if organizations and work itself are living systems – dynamic, ever-changing and interconnected – how can we better understand and design both our digital and physical habitats so that they enable us to do our best work?

These are questions that humankind has been grappling with for centuries, from the way in which our homes are designed, to how our cities are planned, and hospitals, schools and work environments conceived. Indeed, there is a whole field of psychology dedicated to understanding the place–person relationship, called environmental psychology, which recognizes that: 'Our vision of human nature finds expression in the buildings we construct, and these constructions in turn do their silent yet irresistible work of telling us who we are and what we must do.'[73] The online spaces in which we spend so much time are also increasingly subject to research and methodologies based on how they impact us.

Meanwhile, designers exploring how we can better bring the natural world inside, both literally and figuratively, is becoming a more common practice. Social ecologist Stephen Kellert took the concept of biophilia,

Lesser yellownape woodpecker feeding his baby – the habitat that has been selected and crafted by the parent provides ideal protection for the young bird.

An academic study of the relocation process of an IT company of around 50 people, to a new building better suited to the needs of the organization around 'activity-based working' as well as the individual needs of employees, found that **involving employees** in the process for the **design of the new building** was critical to their satisfaction. Because every employee had the chance to be interviewed and complete a detailed survey, 83% were satisfied with their 'participation in the decision-making progress'. Employees perceived greater productivity, cooperation, communication and idea generation, as well as reduced friction, with the new building.[74]

Video game publisher **Ubisoft**'s digital workplace is driven by a robust knowledge management (KM) approach, helping to create a unified experience across its 'best of breed' suite of tools. The Knowledge team, led by **Marc Bramoullé**, has worked hard to understand the different needs of its people and how they work, across the globe. Despite involving a multitude of different platforms and services, this close focus on what people need and want has resulted in a **shared digital habitat** that accommodates the diversity of Ubisoft's work community. The space is given structure through a carefully maintained taxonomy that helps its people to collaborate, seek out experts, and find the right information at the right time, resulting in a 98% satisfaction rate with the KM tools amongst Ubisoft's people.[75]

Nautilus Eco-Resort Biometric Learning Center, Philippines: its mission is zero emission, zero waste and zero poverty. Visionary architect Vincent Callebaut often uses spirals found in nature in creating his biophilic designs for work and life.

popularized by Edward O Wilson as the innate draw of humans to the natural world[24], and created a framework for biophilic design. This was intended to help people better infuse our built environments with elements inspired by and aligned with nature in support of our wellbeing. There are both direct experiences of nature that can be introduced (light, water, plants and natural landscapes), as well as those that bring nature to mind (natural building and design materials, environments that subtly change over time and more natural wayfinding).[76]

Architects such as Gensler have meanwhile developed their own frameworks to help them embed an understanding of our relationship with our environments in their design work. They've identified five 'intentions' that drive human behaviours – tasks, social, discovery, entertainment and aspiration – which the physical environment can be designed to specifically support.[77]

In our digital worlds, specialisms such as User Experience help to shape how online spaces and interfaces are designed to make them more naturally fit our different patterns of behaviour, with knowledge constantly evolving to keep up with new technologies.

The fact that humankind creates its own habitats means that these design choices have a real impact on those who occupy them.

Both our physical and virtual workplaces have gone through radical redesigns during the last decade or so to try and create environments that provide better habitats for us to work in.

Moving dramatically away from the 'cubicle farms' of the 1980s, physical workplace design went in the direction of creating open-plan offices with the intention of facilitating more open and transparent collaboration and communication between people. Strangely though, in pre-COVID-19 times, it had been found that these attempts to bake in interactions and collaboration through creating 'open' spaces can actually lead to people interacting *less*.[78]

The workplace as habitat

The digital workplace has likewise been through an evolution, moving towards ever more personalized experiences and striving to bring together the tools, information and connections people need for their work in a simplified experience. Rather than forcing them to make frustrating and time-consuming journeys through multiple, fragmented and separate digital 'habitats', across a maze of solutions, the goal increasingly is to create integrated experiences that give users the reassuring impression of a single, welcoming, easy-to-navigate environment.

With the pandemic calling the entire idea of a shared physical workplace into question, those organizations best able to adapt to ever-changing physical and virtual workplace needs have been found to be the most effective, healthy and fluid systems.

Our work habitats need to afford us the freedom and flexibility to gravitate to where, when and how we want to work, as we instinctively know what we need at any one time – as long as we are given the freedom to experiment and explore. This may well vary from moment to moment, with individuals in their own preferred physical habitats while sharing a virtual habitat with others. At another time, people may come together in the same physical space to co-work but be occupying different digital spaces.

The physical habitats in which people work vary hugely, with different levels of thought devoted to how well they support those occupying the spaces. Warehouse design, for example, is often focused on supporting the logistics of handling goods and maximizing efficiency, with too little consideration given to how those environments will impact workers from a health and safety perspective.[79] Meanwhile, the design and planning of retail, healthcare, libraries, hospitality venues (in other words, the many different types of non-office location where people also work) are very often dictated first and foremost by how these facilities will serve the public or support efficiency rather than taking into account the comfort and wellbeing of those who work in them.

Before COVID-19, the rise of distributed working, as well as cloud-based technology becoming accessible on mobile devices, had meant that those accustomed to working in offices were already starting to choose their own habitats. The home, cafés, hotel foyers and co-working setups had all become workspaces with the right tools at hand and staff happy to have people working in their space, creating a welcoming environment.

Diversity of work habitats

However, remote working – meaning you get to choose your habitat – hasn't historically been equally accessible across the globe, and research has revealed geographic disparities around whether people have been encouraged to work in the office or not.

Countries such as Singapore and India were found previously to have more office-based workers, due not only to cultural norms but also, for example, to the practicalities of warmer climates – offices are more likely to be air-conditioned and homes in these countries have been found to be typically smaller and more densely populated. The choice and design of the workplace microhabitat is, in essence, influenced by the wider habitat in which it is located.[80]

However, global trends for remote working were completely upended by the pandemic. What became known as the 'great working from home experiment' meant many suddenly became, at least temporarily, homeworkers, finding overnight that 'going to work' now meant the very short commute from the bedroom to wherever in their home could accommodate them with their laptop, phone or tablet.[81] Homes became physical workplaces and the digital workplace became the essential workplace for many – the shared virtual habitat in which they were able to connect with their colleagues.

The 'experiment' revealed the benefits of having more choice over our physical work habitat, favouring those whose work supported flexibility of location, enabled by well-designed digital work habitats. People suddenly found themselves frequently sharing a virtual space in video calls, on collaboration platforms, and through perpetual and instant chats. Personal trainers were able to continue their work with clients virtually as gyms closed, while vets and health practitioners found they could move a number of their consultations online.

Working remotely during a pandemic is not exactly the same as working remotely at other times, but it has helped raise important questions around issues such as wellbeing, boundaries, inclusivity and the timeless need for human contact. Our experience of habitat is not just influenced by the physical space itself but by a whole host of other factors as well. Additional childcare responsibilities, the mental health impact and many other aspects of living through the pandemic reminded us that work can't be easily separated from life; it's all connected.

Out of 21 work-based activities, **Leesman** found that 50,000 respondents to a global survey considered 17 of them to be better from home than in the office, including collaborating on creative work and productivity. However, the same survey found that both connection to colleagues and informal social interactions were felt to be less supported when **working from home** compared to in an office. For people who didn't have a dedicated work room or office at home, their experience of working from home also dropped to a below-average satisfaction rate; under 25s were the most impacted by having to share space with others or not having a specific work-friendly space at home.[68]

Ryan Anderson is Vice President of Global Research & Insights at furniture specialist **Herman Miller** and an expert on the impact of the physical workplace on how we work. Anderson believes that organizations have been rethinking some of the fundamentals about the physical workplace, a process that may be speeded up by COVID-19.[82]

Anderson says: 'We should not think about location as binary – it really isn't about being either an "office worker" or a "remote worker"; it's about enabling people to work from wherever they think is best. Before COVID-19, you would find an average desk might get used 20–30% of a day. People were at home, travelling, in coffee shops, out at clients or suppliers; we've been doing this for a long time.

What happened with COVID is that we were all denied all those options and given just one option to go home. When we begin to transition out, what organizations will realize is that they may have thought about employees as being either assigned to an office or remote teleworkers – but, in fact, it's much blurrier than that Realistically, what we're going to see for a majority of the workforce is more autonomy to choose where they work. And a percentage of that will be in a corporate office facility, as long as these are designed to support important experiences that can't be had elsewhere.'

Infusing human-built habitats with natural elements can help bring the many benefits of nature indoors, much to the benefit of their inhabitants.

While workplace premises are routinely designed to maximize productivity, they can also be configured to support employee health and wellbeing. Sleep is critical for health and workplaces can support this. Organizations such as **Google**, **Nike** and **Ben & Jerry's** have provided 'sleep pods' or spaces – small rooms or standalone furniture – to allow employees to take 'power naps'. **Proctor & Gamble** has introduced lighting systems that dim in the evenings to help regulate melatonin, making it easier for employees working late at night to then sleep when they get home.[83]

Outdoor learning for schoolchildren has been found to benefit their grades and concentration. While this has long been a practice across the African and Asian continents, it's also re-emerging in the West as a rediscovered form of classroom during the pandemic.[84]

Spanish architect Selgascano's Madrid office, situated in a forest just outside the capital. Employees have an eye-level view of the forest floor. With its natural light and situation amongst the trees, this sustainable office gives a strong sense of being integrated with the natural habitat.

Creating more natural work habitats

Many organizations have taken the relative success of the 'working from home experiment' initiated by the COVID-19 pandemic as a signal that they can close their offices by sending their staff home permanently to work solely in the digital workplace, saving the huge budgets that are spent on real estate and equipping physical spaces. But, therein *doesn't* lie the opportunity.

Instead, we should be thinking more broadly about developing natural workspaces positioned throughout the whole ecosystem that is the working world.[1] This is an opportunity to allow us to feel more at ease within our physical and digital environments, across all industries, whether your work can be carried out remotely or you need to be present in person. It's a chance to be creative in terms of the impact of where people are located physically and digitally on local economies, the environment, inclusivity, accessibility, how people's home life is affected, and more.

Even before the pandemic, conversations were starting in various circles that explored how the rise of mobile working could reinvigorate local communities by removing the daily mass exodus into urban centres resulting from the commute to cities.[85]

Offering more flexibility and autonomy in both working hours and place can better support families and caregivers, impacting women in particular. It can also help to redistribute spending more evenly into the towns and areas where people live if they're able to work more

locally and no longer need to commute or move to within reach of a city centre. The role of the city centre itself can be reimagined to support those whose work currently relies on the daily commute. Another effect is that this potentially widens out the talent pool from which people can be hired by an organization.

In essence, expanding what we think of as a working habitat to encompass not just either the office or home, or the virtual, can help act as one of the enablers essential to the overall **Health** of not only the organization but also the wider living system of work.

This is not the end of the office

We know, for example, that the office as a place distinct from home, with its own rhythm and social life, is something that is hugely attractive and important to many people, particularly in the earlier stages of their careers.

This does, however, mark an evolutionary tipping point for the role of the office, as we rethink where work takes place as being something in itself much more dynamic and in line with work as a living system.

As early as 2018, organizations like DWG[86] and CBRE[87] were looking at how work in 2030 and 2040, respectively, may become more focused around 'mixed presence', as Herman Miller's Ryan Anderson described it for the DWG report *Digital Workplace 2030*. The impact of the pandemic on office space means that, for many, the future will have arrived 10 years early.

Campus working, local physical working pods, more advanced and resilient digital workplaces, the role of the office as a meeting

Use of the 'Golden Ratio' in biophilic building design is another subtle way to bring the 'feeling' of nature indoors.[1,2]

place rather than where work gets done exclusively – all were anticipated and are now being accelerated by necessity.[88]

Rather than being approached purely as a cost-saving exercise, the redistribution of where work gets done can be enabled by rethinking how organizations can reallocate that budget to support their people in flexing between habitats.

Do they need more ergonomic furniture? Improved hardware? Digital skills to support remote collaboration and communication? Should knowledge about how to manage distributed teams be enhanced? Is the digital workplace accessible? Would vouchers to spend in local cafés or local co-working spaces be a benefit?

Viewing work as a living system means that organizations can recognize the multitude of physical and virtual habitats their people inhabit day to day, and help them to get the best out of them all rather than just the confines of the office. The digital workplace then becomes 'the essential workplace' – a perpetual, virtual habitat that can be entered from anywhere, at any time.[16]

Alongside this, evidence is mounting on how being physically present in nature supports our **Health** and wellbeing, creating a chance to consider how we bring ourselves closer to natural habitats during our working days.

This more direct connection with nature is being explored through workplace design. A striking example can be found in Spanish architect Selgascano's Madrid office, which is situated in a forest just outside the capital (see pp.55–56). Half of the office is built into the ground and it has an enormous panoramic long window, giving employees an eye-level view of the forest floor. The office is naturally lit through huge skylights. The combined impact is not only a dramatic feeling of being integrated with the natural habitat around but also a highly sustainable office where heat and light are regulated through the building design.[89]

Are we able to better align our working habitats with the seasons in order to be able to work outside? Are future workplaces – whether office, warehouse, hospitality, retail, healthcare or other – better able to harness biophilic design to bring us closer to that natural environment we're so intrinsically drawn towards? We now have the opportunity to create different natural workplaces, where the physical and virtual space are both understood together as 'habitat', designed to properly support people and all their needs.

Ask yourself

- Do you gravitate towards different habitats for your various types of work? Do you have preferences depending on what you're working on?

- What does your ideal physical habitat include and what would you feel like in it? How about your ideal virtual habitat? What feels 'natural' to you?

- What does your ideal habitat look like for in-person co-working and collaboration? What does it look like for virtual co-working and collaboration?

- Has the role of the office changed in your organization or work community? If so, in what ways?

- How do decisions-makers in your organization or work community approach physical and virtual habitats at the moment? Does the approach treat people like machines, or like living beings who are impacted by their environment?

- How could an understanding of 'habitats' be applied to your organization or work community to better support people in their work?

- How could your organization or work community approach physical and virtual habitats to be better designed to blend together, to create more natural workplaces?

Bio diversity

Why diversity is critical to your organization's health

Nature: The variety of life on Earth, or within a particular ecosystem, a high level of which is important as a health indicator

Work: The variety and diversity of people and approaches in an organization across multiple factors, such as experience, expertise, learning style, race and gender

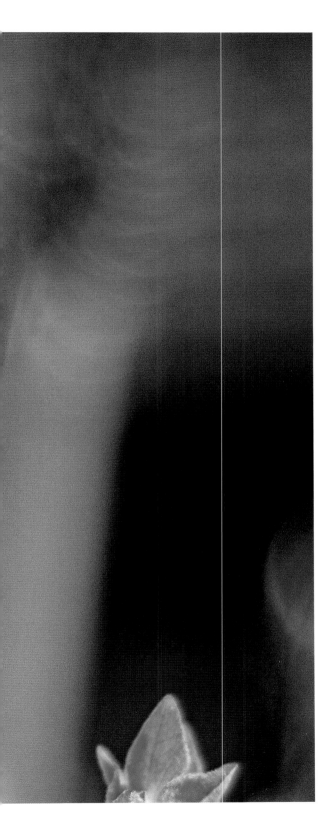

An ecosystem of diversity

The events of 2020 shone a light on just how much more progress is needed in the areas of diversity, inclusion and equity across the work ecosystem, a light that has always been there but too often dimmed in many organizations.

Prior to 2020, some organizations had already started the shift towards creating cultures and habitats where people of all backgrounds feel 'seen, valued and heard', an idea coined by Dr Brené Brown when talking about connection.[90] Movements such as #MeToo and Pride have at different moments served as catalysts for progress, impacting equity work inside organizations.

And as the Black Lives Matter protests took place across the globe in the opening year of our new decade, statistics and testimony about how Black people are prevented from gaining access to work opportunities rang out loud across the airwaves, social media and personal conversations.[91] This is testimony that has always been there – but which has too often gone unheeded.

Similarly, within organizations, the employment experience of Black people is often rife with prejudice and discrimination. Examples of people being subjected to racist microaggressions, having fewer promotion opportunities and needing to meet higher performance expectations are all too common.[92]

Inequity in work has also been reported by other 'non-default' groups, such as those from a range of racial and ethnic minorities, the LGBTQIA+ community[93], those with disabilities[94], and women.[95]

The **UK's Government Digital Service (GDS)** operates an 'Empathy Lab', a physical space where assistive technologies can be tested, but which also raises awareness about accessibility issues. Here, project teams across any government department can assess equipment and use log-in details to experience technologies through the lens of different accessibility issues. Employees, both with and without disabilities, can use the lab to experience the equipment and also for awareness-building exercises.[96]

Dry stone wall Cornwall, UK: provides a sustaining habitat for a wide variey of native thrifts, grasses, lichens, insects and other wildlife.

Separately, the early days of the COVID-19 pandemic suddenly created a global conversation around how well – or poorly – organizations were helping their people to feel they belonged, and were cared for and supported, while living through a mass collective health crisis.

It was observed that organizations consisting of people practising empathy were better able to support and include, for example, those working from home while also having to parent or double as caregivers, and were better equipped to help manage the mental health impacts of living through a pandemic. Empathy helped teams to come together virtually and to collaborate effectively, making

sure everyone was able to participate and contribute.

Normalizing people's different home environments and activities, which were suddenly visible to colleagues through video calls, also emerged as a way of challenging what might formerly have been perceived as either 'professional' or 'unprofessional' at work, throwing a spotlight on the unconscious biases we have around who is and who isn't a capable worker based on things like appearance.[97]

For work communities, the 'baking in' to their DNA of diversity, inclusion, equity and belonging should always have been a crucial element in the health of the organization as well as wider society – but 2020 has highlighted

just how far there still is to go in order to fully establish this particular health factor as a priority in many organizations.

Biodiversity in nature is critical

The importance and power of biodiversity is obvious when we look to the natural world. Wander through any forest or parkland, and you will be surrounded by a rich tapestry of different lifeforms. Working away in the undergrowth will be all manner of insects. Perched in the trees and bushes, birds will be singing and communicating with their various calls and cries. Squirrels will be gathering essential food, rabbits grazing. If it's spring or summer, there'll be butterflies, bees, flowers. In autumn, colourful

The **Timpson Group** in the UK has been training, mentoring, supporting and recruiting both former and current prisoners for more than 15 years. With many people who have served prison sentences often discriminated against in terms of working opportunities, the Timpson's recruitment programme serves to both support this group of people, and create a skilled and particularly dedicated workforce. One employee says that Timpson's has supported her with training, temporary accommodation, company-funded counselling and a loan for a deposit on a home. A culture of inclusivity and belonging is fostered in the company through this, and many other schemes, such as paid time off for a child's first day at school.[98]

berries and sculptural seedheads take centre stage. This variety of life, even in a small stretch of land, is evidence of a healthy ecosystem.

And within this richness of biodiversity, every creature and plant form has its particular role to play, its own niche. Each brings its own specialisms that contribute to keeping the whole ecosystem in balance; the characteristics and needs of the various species all contribute to the **Health** of the entire system. Such biodiversity is essential for life on Earth. With it, the natural world is better able to sustain and stabilize itself and, over time, to withstand, adapt to and recover from **Threats**.[99]

Homogeneity and loss of biodiversity, on the other hand, can put an ecosystem at risk.[100] Within forests, for example, it's been found that simply planting more of the same trees isn't enough to reverse the effects of logging; rather, lessons need to be learned from centuries-old healthy forests that are made up of a mix of different species of tree at various stages of their **Life cycles**, usually growing at varying distances from each other.[101]

Diversity of species, of genetics, age, location, specialism – all are fundamental to the **Health** of an ecosystem if it's to thrive and survive.

The nature of biodiversity in work

Diversity, across all its different meanings – such as expertise, personality, gender, sexuality, race, ethnicity, class, age, disability and faith – likewise allows people, creativity and innovation to thrive. It's essential for the living system of work.

There is already an element of diversity intrinsic to every organization, simply through the mix of skillsets and experiences that exist within its workforce. Different professional perspectives and approaches help to bring a variety of solutions to problem-solving, for example.

Diversity of expertise is therefore something that comes relatively naturally to organizations, as they hire for different roles and then build teams and **Structures** that will draw the best from this range of expertise. Amazingly, this mirrors what has been observed within the natural world: it's been found that animals with different specialisms come together to collaborate, such as the octopus and grouper fish, who will hunt together, combining their specific skills and instinctive hunting practices to help each other succeed in securing their prey.[102]

However, social diversity (or sociodiversity), where people of different ethnicities, race, age, gender, sexual orientation, neurodiversities and disabilities come together within organizations, and across the living system of work, is not yet embedded. This is an element of biodiversity where many organizations struggle, often unintentionally creating homogeneous environments that lack the full diversity of the human experience.

Approaches around diversity of people have a tendency to reflect wider society's overarching attitudes to social equity, with organizations either lagging or just ahead of social norms, despite growing evidence of the benefits to individuals, teams, organizations and

Many organizations have found some success in encouraging and engaging with internal employee resource groups (ERGs) that represent different communities of employees, typically based on race, gender, sexual orientation, age, disability or background (for example, military veterans). When these groups are able to actively influence diversity and inclusion policies and initiatives, positive results can ensue; for example, **T-Mobile** reported significantly higher retention rates with employees who participated in such groups.[103]

Richemont, the owner of several global luxury brands, such as Cartier, has created a global digital workplace environment in which customized versions of its platform reflect the identity of the specific brands while still incorporating global features and content.[104]

communities, not to mention the effect on equity across wider society.

Within the mechanistic view of work and the organization, uniformity and homogeneity are easier to manage, with everything tending to fit neatly into predefined frameworks that don't need to evolve and flex. To those with this mindset, making room for diversity can seem more difficult, as introducing diversity frequently challenges traditional power dynamics and **Structures**.

The nurturing of sociodiversity is therefore too often reduced to little more than a tick-box activity and an after-thought to how the organization is formed, grows and regenerates. For example, policies such as affirmative action where quotas for hiring based on gender and race are identified, have narrowly focused on numbers rather than also considering the experiences people have once they are within the organization. As we learned from the forest regeneration example, more trees don't necessarily lead to a healthy forest.

There is also often a desire within global organizations to foster a 'one company' culture in terms of values and practices. While there are some deep benefits to this approach, particularly in creating shared **Purpose** and **Roots**, it can unintentionally diminish diversity by minimizing the benefits of localized cultures and nuances. As we saw in the example of different foxes in **Habitats**, adaptations to local environments are an integral part of nature. A healthy global/local balance is one where the local is celebrated and harnessed while still supporting the shared purpose required to drive the whole organization.

Diversity benefits all

In the living system mindset of work and the organization, biodiversity is seeded from the beginning. Recognizing intersections of identity and experience, and not having a 'one size fits all' approach, is intrinsic to who the organization is, regardless of its industry. From a small design agency to a global logistics company, biodiversity can be allowed to flourish for the benefit of all.

Having a diverse workforce that is empowered to work together and build **Relationships** has a positive effect on decision-making, information-processing, productivity, creativity and innovation within the organization, ultimately affecting growth and the bottom line. It also impacts employment opportunities across society, with all the socioeconomic knock-on effects that entails.[105]

Through cultures that fail to create inclusive **Habitats** and don't address unconscious bias in hiring practices, organizations are failing to enable their people to be and do their best, and missing out on talent altogether. What's more, people are often forced to leave key aspects of themselves at the door of the workplace if they wish to belong, which in itself takes up mental bandwidth that could otherwise be directed towards the work they have been hired to do.[106]

The organization as a living system – indeed, work as a living system – needs biodiversity, in all its forms, as a critical health indicator that goes beyond just the numbers of who's in the room.

One of the ways in which US software company **Adobe** balances its global identity with localized diversity is through its habitats. It has transitioned from having a global standard for all its offices to actively encouraging each office to reflect and represent its city or country location in terms of design – while still feeling like an Adobe space. So, the Paris workspace is specifically designed to feel like it's Adobe in France, rather than a generic Adobe space that could just as well be on the West Coast of the US.[1]

Coral reef and fishes, Red Sea, Egypt. Coral reefs are essential for biodiversity in the seas and hugely under threat. The diversity in a company must be protected at all times.

Do you feel like you belong?

We saw in **Habitats** how important someone's digital and physical environment is in supporting their work and in making sure they feel enabled and empowered.

Combining an understanding of **Habitats** with an appreciation of biodiversity helps us to recognize that not everyone's experience of those habitats will necessarily be the same.

This is why culture is so important. The behaviours, values and social norms you encounter while in these spaces – which tell you, amongst other things, what is acceptable and what isn't – will impact how you feel while in those **Habitats**, combined with the other signals you are receiving from how the spaces have been designed.[107] An organization's cultural habitat tells you whether you belong or whether you don't.

There are numerous signals you might pick up that can make you feel as if you don't belong – which, in turn, can impact performance as well as mental or physical **Health**. These could include:

- A lack of recognition and support may mean you don't feel valued.
- You may feel you have to hide, reduce or change facets of who you are through 'code-switching' if these are perceived to be 'unprofessional' (such as how you speak or dress).
- Your autonomy over how you wish or need to work may be discouraged through an inflexible work environment.

- Not having the tools you need to do your work could mean you feel your role isn't valued.
- Not seeing people like you in positions of power or influence may make you feel you are not suited to those positions yourself.

Signals like these can make an individual feel as if they don't have their own niche within the organization's **Habitats** – and such a feeling of acceptance is crucial if diversity across all its different aspects is to be allowed to flourish rather than to be suppressed.

Creating cultures of belonging

Understanding and expertise related to how best to create inclusive and equitable cultures are evolving. Unconscious bias training is one technique that has been tried; however, to be effective, this has to be embedded within a broader, longer-term programme of work. This is key, as it's been found that, when delivered in isolation or as a tick-box activity, there may be short-term benefits but no lasting positive impact on the beliefs and behaviours of an individual.[108] This serves as a useful reminder that any efforts to create inclusive cultures need to cover a variety of activities and that there are no 'quick fixes'.

Fostering inclusive diversity across different aspects of work is undoubtedly challenging, whether this refers to diversity of expertise, demographics, geography, or any other way in which variety is deliberately sought and celebrated. Not having a homogenous workforce means that empathy and

Spanish fashion retailer **INDITEX**, owner of the Zara brand among others, actively ensures that its supply chain adheres to various sustainable policies covering many aspects such as human rights, equal pay, responsible management, caring for the environment and ethical trading. It does this through a published set of standards and a rolling programme of evaluation and training, partially driven through local platforms for dialogue involving the company, suppliers and local stakeholders.[109]

Wildflower meadow, Carpathian Mountains, Romania, including a mix of ox-eye daisies, harebells, dandelions and clover. Diversity creates a healthy organization.

understanding become even more crucial. However, efforts in this area have been found to pay off. The perceived tensions that can flow from different ideas and backgrounds coming together can result in better decision-making and problem-solving – so long as everyone feels psychologically safe to fully express themselves.[110]

And what's more, creating an inclusive workplace that celebrates diversity of expression has been found to benefit everyone.[111] Not only can it lead to everyone within the organization feeling empowered, it can also result in a more diverse set of services and products, expanding the organization's reach of who they serve.

The signals that help to foster a sense of belonging, cement trust in one another and encourage empathy are numerous. The very fact of having a diverse workforce, in all its senses, can mean that no one is made to feel tokenized

Oxfam International is a confederation of 20 affiliate organizations working across more than 65 countries. This structural and geographic spread means the workforce is extremely diverse, but it also leads to challenges common to many such organizations. One such challenge is to ensure equal representation and influence from all countries within the network.

In 2017, Oxfam set up an instance of Workplace from Facebook across its entire network. This has had a significant positive impact on collaboration and culture by removing some of the barriers to a truly diverse network from working together as well as it could. **Dianna Langley**, the former Digital Workplace Manager, explains: 'We needed a way that anyone from any country or any affiliate could make a request from a network of 10,000 colleagues… With Workplace you can "show up" to a conversation with a lot less organizational,

cultural or hierarchical baggage. The way people are displayed doesn't focus on their job title or location or team. It all feels like a more equal space.'

This has dramatically increased the confidence of people across the network to reach out to colleagues. Other barriers around language and formality can be removed too; for example, the auto-translation option means people can simply post in their native language within the conversations.

Workplace has continued to have a positive impact, with the ability for anybody to participate and use the platform, regardless of country, language, organization or place in the hierarchy. Anyone can post or form a group, while Oxfam's Internal Communications team can curate highlights from contributions to ensure that news reflects what is happening right across the network.[65]

or just a 'diversity hire' (in itself a misguided idea, as diversity only ever exists within groups; a single person cannot in themselves be diverse).

For internal communications, the stories that are told – by whom, with what language, and in what channel or medium – can affect whether people feel included or excluded. When social networking tools are used to good effect, for example, they can support the communication and collaboration that help drive inclusion.

Managers and colleagues who truly support each other, and show care and empathy, can build better understanding and trust as a team, helping to create inclusive cultures, where people feel they belong and are cared for. During the pandemic, CEOs have been recording frequent messages for employees and opening dialogue. Satya Nadella, CEO of **Microsoft**, sent a message to all employees saying 'deep empathy and understanding for each other's situations is needed now more than ever.[112]

As regards collaboration, whether in person or online, everyone can be supported to participate by using a multitude of different collaboration methods. Tools and ways of working that allow people to oscillate between working alone, collaborating asynchronously and coming together in real-time, for example, can be crucial for both participation from a variety of different people and better-quality outcomes.[113]

Supporting flexible and remote working patterns, if implemented thoughtfully, can allow people not only to work in ways that help them be their best in work, but can also have a positive impact on their non-work lives through better balance. Parents and caregivers, for example, benefit hugely from being able to work more flexibly and it can enable them to be part of the work ecosystem. For example, the extended homeworking patterns driven by the pandemic lockdown have facilitated greater flexible working for some. Surveys suggest that up to 90% of parents and carers want their employers to retain these 'flexible working practices' once the COVID-19 crisis is resolved.[114]

Digital and physical workplaces created to be truly accessible and usable can also help improve the experience for all if baked in from the start, through effective people-centred research and design.

And, within recruitment, making an effort to extend beyond the usual talent pools from which an organization normally recruits, noticing the different types of bias that affect decision-making around hires, being mindful of how the idea of 'culture fit' can actually exclude people from different backgrounds from being considered as a suitable candidate, can all contribute to an organization presenting a welcoming environment in which diversity can flourish.[108]

Diversity within the living system of work doesn't stop at the organization's boundaries either. Access to education, opportunities for

Biodiversity of animal species with their wonderful variety of size, colour, purpose and adaptations to different habitats is essential to the healthy functioning of our planet's ecosystem. More than 16,000 species are currently in danger of extinction.

Inclusion and diversity has become a core part of **Dow**'s business strategy, involving a governance structure, vision statement, key performance indicators (KPIs), areas of focus and clear strategy implementation plans. Its annual *Shine Inclusion Report* documents the organization's progress against these goals, with particular focus on its seven foundation pillars: governance, customers, talent, people leaders, suppliers, communities and reputation. Three different **Inclusion Councils** help set the strategy and ensure implementation across the company, working closely with its ERG network, of which there are 10, covering racial and ethnic inclusion, women, disability, mature workers, disabilities, LGBTQ+ and new employees.[116]

work experience, availability of appropriate technology, the effects of poverty, plus a whole host of other socioeconomic elements, all impact whether equity is experienced or not.[115]

Even once steps have been taken towards diversity, inclusion and belonging, **Threats** can emerge that risk undoing any progress that has been made. There is already evidence that one of the impacts of the COVID-19 pandemic has been to affect the number of women in the workforce, through factors such as their being disproportionately the casualties of job losses and having to take on extra childcare and home-schooling responsibilities.[117] Even once a commitment has been made to prioritize the biodiversity of an organization, constant vigilance and feedback loops are needed to ensure this remains a priority and that appropriate actions are being taken.

For individuals, teams, organizations and the wider living system of work to all thrive, true biodiversity, where people feel and know they belong, is crucial at all levels. Without it, social equity isn't possible; social mobility can't happen; citizen participation is diminished. The full spectrum of services and products that people need and want isn't available, organizations become stagnant – and people's ability to succeed in work is severely challenged.

Allowing biodiversity to flourish means that all have their niche within the living system of work, where they are able to harness the full breadth and depth of their strengths, experiences, knowledge and expertise, serving themselves, their colleagues, the organization and, ultimately, wider society.

Ask yourself

- Do you feel as though you belong in your organization or work community and that you can bring your full self to work? If not, which parts of yourself do you feel you need to minimize or hide, and why?

- How do you and people in your organization or work community understand and define diversity, inclusion, equity and belonging at the moment?

- Do you have a shared understanding and articulation of how important this area is to the health of your organization or work community and its people? If not, what could that look like?

- How do people in your organization or work community demonstrate through their words and actions that there is a culture of inclusion and belonging, and that people's voices and opinions matter? How could you do this better?

- Do you and people in your organization or work community feel psychologically safe enough to raise issues related to diversity, inclusion, equity and belonging? If not, what consequences are people scared of?

- How empathetic are people in your organization or work community to each other?

- Are there people in wider society that you don't see represented at all levels in your organization or work community? If not, why could that be? Are there unspoken assumptions about who 'belongs' and who doesn't? How could that change?

Relationships

What story is told by the nature of interactions in your organization?

Nature: The way in which two or more things are connected, or the state of being connected

Work: The interconnections, behaviours and communication in work

Meerkats are found in the deserts and grasslands of Botswana and Namibia, Africa. A sentry stands on duty scanning for predators, while his so-called 'mob' hunt for prey. Intricate and equitable relationships help create healthy and vibrant workplaces.

Unspoken patterns

Sometimes there is gentle teasing, but in **DWG** we rarely swear in our conversations with each other. We can only assume that most of the team do swear in their personal lives, but this practice is an unspoken DWG norm. We also have certain shared expectations regarding respectful communication, both verbal and written. For example, it tends to sound warning bells when there's an instance of a more senior person talking down to someone more junior. In our experience across the past 20 years of DWG, a pattern of behaviour where someone treats their colleagues at any level with disrespect has been the most common reason for that person leaving, far outstripping problems with performance or capability.

Now, that might make DWG sound like a sanctified space of morality, more akin to a convent than a consulting firm, but this is not the case. The culture, atmosphere and practices are mostly described by our people (and clients, as there is often little to separate the two) as 'informal, light-hearted, intelligent, conscientious, supportive' and yes, 'respectful'. The absence of swearing is not a puritanical edict but closely connected to maintaining respectful and inclusive ways of working.

These DWG habits are about creating and maintaining healthy, trusting, resilient and natural relationships in work.

Thriving naturally through connections

To be part of the natural world, whether in a forest or the desert or any other ecosystem, is to be entwined in a huge network of relationships linking creatures, places and objects – a network through which energy, matter, knowledge, information and much more constantly flow. All is connected, from the smallest of insects through to the largest mountain range. It's all just a matter of scale and perspective.

Some of these relationships are easy to spot. The monkeys and apes who live in familial groups, grooming each other (*see pp.77–78*) and playing together to build ties, have their own highly developed internal politics and family norms, and are an easily relatable example of how relationships between social animals can function. Another example of how these relationships manifest in the natural world can be found in meerkat clans; for example, studies into their behaviour have found that they take turns at standing sentry while others in the group forage for food (*see opposite*).

Many of these complex behavioural relationships have been uncovered (and are frequently brilliantly captured and explained in natural history documentaries). We have already heard about the collaborative hunting efforts of the octopus and grouper fish.[113] Countless other examples exist, such as the teamwork of

During the COVID-19 lockdown, although the UK restaurant chain **Honest Burgers** had to put many of its staff on furlough, it made efforts to support them by putting together a 'stay connected' timetable of online events – as part of it, the CEO even ran fitness sessions from his house dressed in 1980s gear. [118]

"Everything within nature exists in relation to a multitude of different elements, creating an interconnected web of dependencies."

ostriches and zebras, who will travel together to keep themselves safe from their shared predators – ostriches have poor hearing and a weak sense of smell, while zebras have bad eyesight, so they band together to support each other and draw on their complementary strengths (*see pp.75–76*).[119] There are also relationships that help animals to learn from each other, seen for example amongst elder orcas, who 'coach' younger orcas in their pods on hunting techniques.[120]

And we can observe more competitive relationships too, such as amongst Adélie penguins, who are not above secretively stealing rocks for nest-building from their neighbours while the unsuspecting victims of theft are looking the other way.[121]

But relationships aren't just found amongst animals. Everything within nature exists in relation to a multitude of different elements, creating an interconnected web of dependencies. Plants have a relationship with the Sun (*see p.166*) and the earth as sources of energy and nutrients. What's more, they have a relationship with each other, such as in how trees communicate with one another, as we saw in **Roots**. They also have a relationship with the insects and animals and weather patterns that help them to spread their seeds to survive – and with the creatures that feed upon them.

Many of these are examples of 'mutualism', interactions between those of either the same or different species that benefit both, and on which the natural world is so dependent.[122]

Animals have been found to have relationships with both objects and places.

Sea otters, for example, can have a 'favourite' rock that they will keep, using it both as a tool and for 'juggling' (*see p.81*).[123] And many animals, from mammals to birds to fish, regularly **Migrate** between familiar **Habitats** for mating and food as the seasons shift.

While various boundaries can be conceptually drawn around groups based on different types of relationship, these are always malleable, expanding and contracting depending on how narrow or wide a lens you use. You can pick out a family group by setting the frame around social and blood ties. A predator–prey relationship between two different species can be identified as you pull back a little wider. Zoomed out further still, the full ecosystem comes into view, encompassing all the multiple relationships that might exist in, say, for example, a coral reef.

And so, when we perceive a living system at any level within nature, we are ultimately looking at a rich and diverse network of relationships.

Living relationships in work

The world of work as a living system teems with the same networks as nature. They've always been at the heart of how work gets done, through the movement and use of resources, sharing of expertise, competition and collaboration. However, the health of those different types of relationship has varied over time, depending on who – and what – is and isn't valued, and who does and doesn't have power.

The relationships we value, notice and group together within the living system of work, have a huge impact. They influence how effectively

As far back as 2008, the 'Hot Chilli' programme at **Unilever** paired up junior IT managers as mentors to 100 top senior managers for one-on-one sessions covering topics such as virtual team working.[124] This approach is often referred to as 'reverse mentoring' and receives great feedback, where typically senior management or older employees buddy up with younger, more digitally savvy employees. The younger employees demonstrate how to use digital and social tools to improve managers' confidence, knowledge and awareness, and make them more digitally dexterous. In a good scheme, the benefits of the reverse mentoring are two-way, with the younger employees gaining visibility, learning and job shadowing opportunities from the senior managers. For example, in **Scottish Government**'s successful 'Digital Friends' initiative, the scheme is explicitly designed to benefit both parties.[125]

people are able to collaborate with one another, who they see themselves as being in competition with, who they learn from, who they listen to, who they consider will be affected by decisions. And they impact how an organization treats its people.

Does leadership and management maintain the industrialized power dynamic of regarding people simply as 'resources' to be managed along with other 'assets', focused solely on maximizing efficiency and productivity with an 'us and them' mindset? Or does the C-suite view its relationship with people across the organization as one of mutual respect, where leaders and managers are there to empower and enable, and are in the service of their colleagues?

People with a living system mindset are more likely to nurture empathetic, empowering relationships with their colleagues and also with those outside the organization, traits that are essential too for supporting **Biodiversity**.

Signals about which relationships are valued and which aren't can be received through the ways in which digital and physical work **Habitats** are designed and experienced, as well as people's relationships with those environments. Such signals might include:

- people being empowered through their workplace and culture to have relationships with the leadership and feeling their voice is being heard
- the employee experience being designed so that people's relationship with the organization is one of mutual respect, rather than of toxicity and abuse

- people having the tools they need to connect and collaborate with one another
- non-work focused interactions being enabled to flourish, such as through lunches, sports, music groups, and more
- respectful behaviours towards one another being encouraged and rewarded, rather than those that cause harm.

In addition, the relationships that an organization and its people have with their surrounding communities and natural environment have historically been valued far less than relationships with stakeholders and customers. This can in turn, for example, impact social equity and ecological conservation.

Ultimately, the relationships that are valued, and those that aren't, can speak volumes about who an organization is at its **Roots**.

Relationships as the basis for collaboration and communication

The nature of our relationships with our colleagues impacts how effectively we collaborate and communicate together. How we treat each other through our relationships will dictate whether we trust each other, seem valued, and feel safe enough to share ideas, learn together, create together and fail together.

To nurture **Biodiversity**, organizations need to value the full range and depth of relationships that exist between their people, supported through elements such as shared **Purpose** and sensitively designed **Habitats**.

African Bush, Etosha National Park, Namibia: ostritches and zebras work as a team, drawing on each other's different capabilities, to remain safe against their various predators.

75

Although COVID-19 has changed attitudes to face-to-face meetings, they are still very important. **Dr Nicola Millard**, Principal Innovation Partner, **BT**, comments: 'We will always need face-to-face interaction because there's something very unique about it. In some senses, it's almost a luxury. When we do a face-to-face meeting we need to make sure it ticks all the boxes, not only considering the impact on the environment, but also if it's going to be productive. There also are some real subtleties around how different cultures view relationships, with high-touch and low-touch cultures. So there may be a need to do face-to-face simply because culturally it's more acceptable.'126

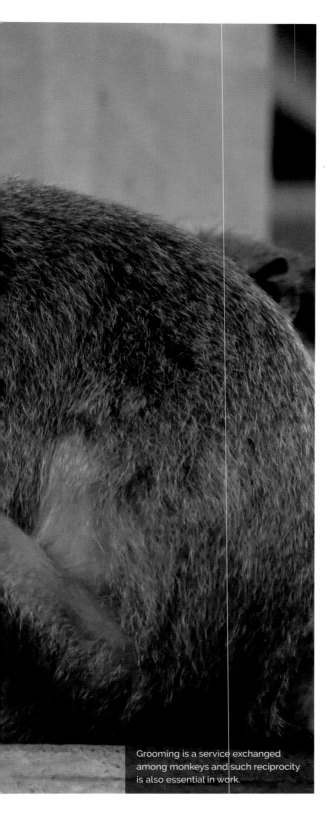

Grooming is a service exchanged among monkeys and such reciprocity is also essential in work.

The COVID-19 pandemic has in many cases had a transformative impact on the relationship between the leaders of organizations and their employees, even though this process of strengthening relationships is not always easy. Many CEOs having moved towards a more empathetic and personal style of communications.

Creating habitats that support relationships

The appearance of digital social networks in our personal lives in the late 2000s gave rise to a parallel conversation around networks within the organization, bringing a renewed focus on the different types of relationship that exist across the work living system and how these can be better understood and supported.

Concepts such as 'weak ties' and 'strong ties', drawn from sociology and social network theory, suddenly became cornerstones in the case for enterprise social networks and the use of 'Web 2.0' tools in work.[127] The technology seemed to make visible the volume of conversations, collaboration and knowledge sharing that was already taking place beyond the formal organizational structures of departments and teams.

As a result, the ideas of 'social business' or the 'connected company' or 'networked company' were increasingly spoken about. This flurry of thinking and activity that bubbled up recognized the myriad networks of informal relationships that exist within organizations and the full diversity of the nature of those relationships.

Automattic is a global software company with over 1,000 employees. It is a fully virtual organization with no physical premises. However, the company strongly believes in the importance of staff meeting in person and each year spends millions of dollars on a global week-long conference, which the great majority of staff attend.

CEO **Matt Mullenweg** writes: 'The Grand Meetup is our chance to get to know people behind the Slack avatars and build relationships that can carry us through the other 51 weeks of the year, when we're working from more than 65 countries. It's so much easier to hear the nuance of someone's chat messages or p2p posts if you've hung out with them at Harry Potter World, or learnt about their family, pets and hobbies during a flash talk.'[128] Automattic has also analysed communication before and after one of its annual Grand Meetups and found that interactions between staff in work-related online channels increased 'drastically and significantly' after the event.[129]

It is now standard for building design to be oriented to supporting relationships, both within the workplace but also beyond it. When furniture design company **Vitsœ** designed its new HQ and production building near Leamington Spa, UK, many considerations such as cost, sustainability, being located near its suppliers, integration with the natural habitat, health and wellbeing, and even the cultural heritage of the area, were major factors in the eventual build. But supporting relationships was also key.[130]

Mark Adams, Vitsœ's Managing Director, writing about the new building in 2017, said: 'Internally this building is about visibility and serendipity; bumping into each other; fewer meetings… Externally, this building is open to its community. It has windows so that we can see out to the greenery, but also our future employees can see in – and be tempted. This building is designed to be part of the community that has welcomed Vitsœ so warmly.'

Furniture design company Vitsœ's new HQ in England: the design encourages ad hoc conversations and reduces the need for formal meetings (*photo taken before COVID-19 required social distancing measures*).

We learned that organizations don't need to *become* 'networked' or 'living systems' in terms of their relationships – because they already are. However, this can still be challenging as sometimes the tools available are limited to shaping more mechanistic interactions.

The good news though is that the way in which our physical and digital work **Habitats** are being designed is increasingly focused on how they can best support the relationships and interactions we have and need with each other for work, such as through Herman Miller's Modes of Work[131] and ClearBox's Activity Based Working (ABW) framework for the digital workplace.[132] For Herman Miller, workplaces need to support interactions such as incidental and impromptu chats, more purposeful conversations, the ability to co-create, as well as enabling the individual to contemplate and focus alone.

In 2020, when usage of Microsoft Teams rocketed due to the COVID-19 pandemic, questions around how it was different to Yammer were answered with reference to the different relationships each support: either 'inner loops' for MS Teams (who you work with closely, day to day) or 'outer loops' for Yammer (those you come across less regularly, or your 'weak ties').[133]

Relationships beyond organizational boundaries

The relationships through which work gets done don't stop at the boundaries of the organization, of course. There are relationships with those who supply materials, products, tools and services to the organization – as well as with those who benefit from the services and products the organization creates. Other relationships include those with the families and friends of workers; the communities in which organizations are located; the environment; and the schools and educational systems teaching the next generations of people.

Recognizing the organization and the wider elements of work as parts of the same living system means being able to see how networks of relationships stretch both outwards to and inwards from the 'outside world' to the organization.

A digital workplace that is designed to be accessible 24/7 can both accommodate and impact people's familial ties, for example. Supporting a 'work from anywhere' style can impact people's relationships with their local communities. Choices made about travel and suppliers influence relationships with the environment and nature.

While not every decision can positively impact every single relationship that exists within the living system of work, thought can be given to which relationships are valued in decision-making and ways in which these relationships can potentially be supported. Trying to anticipate any unintended consequences from the choices made by people within organizations can be helped by being attentive to which relationships between the organization and society are included in discussions.

A number of different frameworks exist that can be adapted by organizations to help them expand out which relationships they value and consider.

Small clawed otter playing with a stone. Many otters have a favourite stone they store in their underarm pockets and use to open clams. People likewise have preferred tools that they use for their work, often leading to more personalized workplaces.

In 2018, strategic and service designer Cassie Robinson gathered together seven different frameworks that help expand thinking from 'human-centred design' (i.e. focused on the individual) to a mindset focused on the different relationships impacted by design decisions.[46]

Examples include **Relational Design**, which helps consider and design for the interdependencies at different scales (such as an individual, a community, an organization) and **Ecosystem Design**, which helps organizations coordinate their design efforts within the context of their ecosystems.

STEEPLE analysis, for example, which takes in social, technological, environmental, economic, political, legal and ethical factors that impact the organization, can be flipped to consider how decisions made by the organization in turn impact its relationships with those elements.[134]

The Doughnut model, developed by economist Kate Raworth, can likewise be adapted to help organizations consider how their work and decisions relate to social and ecological impacts, such as gender and social equality, or air pollution.[135] Improved parental leave, for example, where both fathers and mothers are fully supported to take meaningful time away from work, safe in the knowledge they'll be able to return, can contribute to gender equality both at home and in the workplace.

A broadened understanding of an organization's relationships can become a powerful force when combined with a deeper understanding of the **Purpose** of work and the organization within society.

As we saw earlier in **Roots**, food company **Leon UK** was able quickly to establish relationships with a network of different restaurants, suppliers, delivery services and celebrities around the shared **Purpose** of providing meals to frontline health workers during the peak of the COVID-19 pandemic.[67] Similar collaborative partnerships were quickly formed, putting aside thoughts of competition for a greater purpose.

There is an increasing list of global 'wicked' problems facing life on Earth, experienced acutely at the local level. In order to address them, we can ultimately see the entirety of the system of work as one that is dynamic and alive, and thriving through the relationships that can be formed between people when there's a shared **Purpose** bringing them together.

The collaborative relationships that can form within an organization can ultimately likewise be formed between organizations, if people are empowered to do so. All it can take is a shift in focus and a redrawing of the line that surrounds different relationships.

Ask yourself

- How do your words and actions demonstrate which work relationships you value?

- Are there people and areas who both impact and are impacted by your work, with whom you don't have a very strong – or any – relationship, across and outside of your organization or work community? If so, why not and what steps can you take to better establish those relationships?

- To what extent do you take responsibility for showing what healthy, reciprocal relationships look like across your work living system?

- What sort of relationships do the physical and work habitats, and culture, of your organization or work community enable? Are these well-balanced relationships?

- To what extent does your organization or work community display strong relationships with its people, and with its external environment? How do your leaders role model what is and isn't acceptable in their relationships?

- What stands in the way of healthy relationships within your organization or work community?

Structures

Designing your organization as a living system

Nature: The arrangement of and relations between the parts or elements of something complex

Work: How the relationships between people are grouped together to form the ecosystem of an organization

Army ants build bridges with their bodies, allowing other ants to cross a gap to expand the range of their foraging activity. Similarly, innovative structures in work often enable outcomes that are impossible for any individual to achieve alone.

Emergent structures in a digital age

In 2012, UK bank **Barclays** decided it wanted to go on a journey of digital transformation. After the 2008 financial crash, all banks (as Barclays saw it) were mired in reputational collapse and needed to rebuild their reputations and business models.

The leadership team asked its then Strategic Transformation Director, Steven Roberts, to lead the initiative. The way in which he approached this daunting challenge and what was subsequently created is a fascinating story of working with a living system structure and approach.

Instead of hiring a new team from outside Barclays, Steven tapped into his own network within the bank and sought out long-standing colleagues who were both well-networked across the bank but also understood the culture and how to get things done. Steven wanted to work within the existing system and adapt it for the future.

From there, the concept of 'Digital Eagles'[136] was realized by creating a group of digital evangelists who could bring new technologies and ideas to this conservative financial services giant that was founded in 1896. Again, his approach was unexpected. He asked his team for a list of 20 younger people from anywhere in the bank, who they felt could become digital trainers and change agents. He told the 20 people selected they could become Barclays' first ever Digital Eagles, should they wish to. This sounded fun, exciting and gave the young employees status in the bank.

This organic way of shaping a new structure within the bank then went further, as each Eagle was asked to recruit a further 20 willing Eagles who they felt had the right stuff for this journey. And on it went – within a few months there were 3,000 Digital Eagles, each on a mission of digital transformation. This emergent community had grown ground-up through a networked non-hierarchical and non-traditional approach.

At the same time, Barclays gave all the retail branch staff an Apple iPad in the then largest ever purchase of iPads, with some 11,500 devices distributed across the network.[137] The Digital Eagles programme has transformed Barclays, with digital literacy brought via the Eagles to staff and customers, and even to non-customers. Hackathons, labs, digital driving licences, life skills and coding for children have followed in turn, helping to address the 'digital divide' of technological inequality.

This is a powerful example of one way of structuring something new in an organization in an organic and living system way. It brings with it challenges but contains a flow, ease and energy that top-down mandates fail to capture. In engaging the 20 original Eagles, the energy and ambition of this younger cohort was harnessed, as it was again when they were later tasked with approaching their own 20 new Eagles.

Structures for survival

Witnessing social structures manifest within the animal kingdom can be a thing of mesmerizing beauty; for example, the intricate coordinated patterns created by sometimes hundreds of thousands of starlings gathering together to fly in unison and appearing to create waves in the sky, known as a 'murmuration' (*see pp.89–90*).[138]

In the ocean, schools of fish will come together to form large, glittering structures as they move through the water, appearing almost to be a single organism as they create bait balls for defence (*see p.95*)[139] or 'tornadoes' for courtship.[140]

Amongst mammals, we can discern numerous examples of structures that help to organize roles and **Relationships**, such as within the matriarchal structures formed by orcas, wolves and big cats.

Perhaps some of the most obvious examples of natural social structures are among ants, termites and bees, which organize in tightly defined social groups, with clear work roles and purposes allocated to each member of the colony or hive.[141,142]

Even when different species encounter each other, social structures can help support cooperation over shared turf. For example, it has been observed that foraging termites and ants sharing the same **Habitat** will combine to create a double 'wall' of soldiers (one formed of termites, the other of ants), which helps to separate the parallel trails being used by each species' workers.[143]

In each of these examples, the actions of an individual, seemingly autonomous, combines with the actions of other individuals to create something bigger, a structure that together has its own **Purpose** and strength larger than that which any single individual is able to achieve alone.

These structures help bring individuals together for safety from predators and the elements, or for greater foraging and hunting success. They can also help foster social learning and information sharing.

The behaviours that we see unfold within these structures, and indeed how the structures themselves form, are emergent; they're dependent on so many different factors, such as climate, **Habitat**, the presence of predators, availability or scarcity of food, and the cumulative effect of all the separate decisions made by individuals.[144]

The constant influx of new information from the local environment that needs assimilating and reacting to, based on the collective experience of the group, all impacts how the social structure ultimately behaves; there is no external or separate conductor dictating what individuals should be doing minute to minute or over a longer period.

Different species lend themselves to various structures, group behaviours and **Relationships**; an ant colony works differently to a pride of lions. But within all, elements such as emergence, feedback loops, communication, optimum size, localized knowledge, collective **Intelligence**

In a wonderful example of a disciplined structure that can also respond to the needs of individuals, **Emperor penguins** create huge, circular huddles for warmth, rotating roughly every 60 seconds to make sure all get a turn within the heart of the huddle – but when this leads to the penguins at the centre overheating the huddle responds by allowing them to move out before then reforming the tightly knit structure.[145]

Emperor penguin breeding colony huddling together for warmth during the Polar night, Atka Bay, Antarctica.

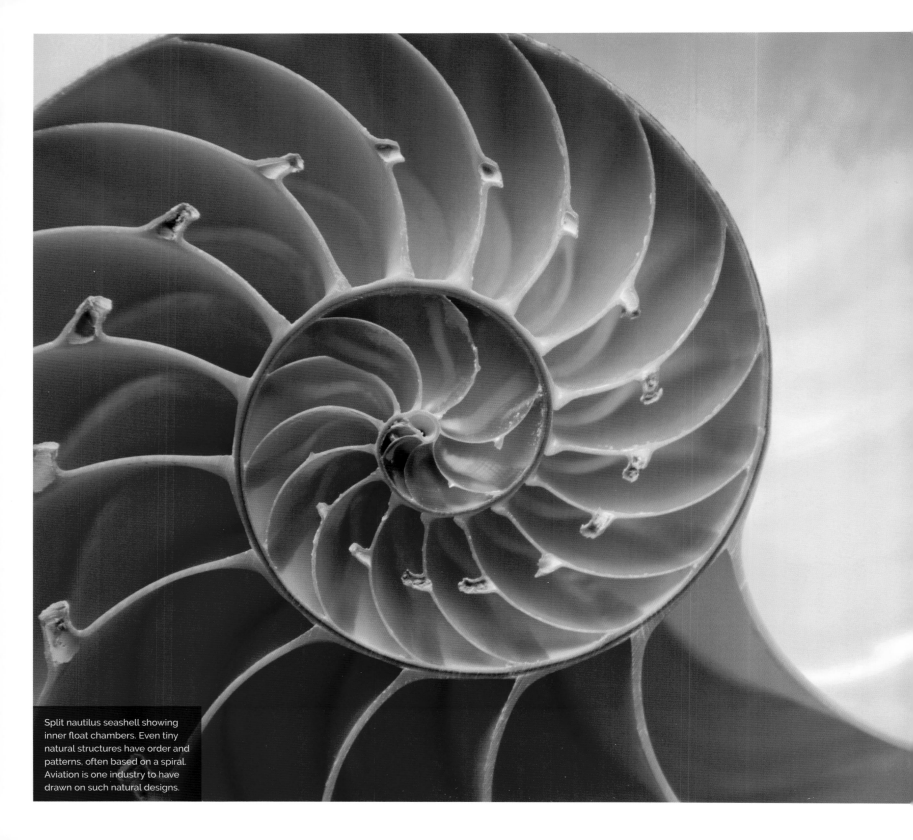

Split nautilus seashell showing inner float chambers. Even tiny natural structures have order and patterns, often based on a spiral. Aviation is one industry to have drawn on such natural designs.

A Dutch model for social care, named 'Buurtzorg', has shown how structuring teams of nurses to have more autonomy by allowing decision-making to take place within a network of small, local teams has improved the quality of healthcare for patients.[146]

British anthropologist, **Robin Dunbar**, concluded that the 'natural' size of a social structure that humans could cognitively handle was 150 meaningful relationships. Beyond that, the group would start to deteriorate and potentially splinter into smaller groups. Evidence for the longevity of this number has been found throughout the history of the human race and across a vast array of different community types.[147] While the specific number 150 has been contested, it's interesting to note that SMEs – organizations consisting of up to roughly 250 people – are thought to make up more than 95% of firms globally and to employ roughly 60–70% of the workforce.[148]

and learning play a role in the overall success of the structure and, ultimately, of the individuals within it.

So many other examples of structure within nature exist, whether through the rhythm and cadence of time in **Life cycles** and seasons, or within the physical, such as the golden spiral of shells (*see opposite*) and fractal patterns of plants. Within a seemingly fragmented natural world, structure thrives, from the smallest cell up to the Solar System itself and beyond.

Organizations as structured relationships

The very concept of an 'organization' has structure inherent within it. As in nature, organizations bring together diverse **Relationships** and specialisms to help achieve a shared **Purpose** that wouldn't be possible or at least as effective if pursued by individuals alone.

The way in which those **Relationships** are formed, nurtured and brought together ultimately helps to create communities of shared interests and **Purpose**. These are structures of relationships through which resources, knowledge, trust, emotional support and collective wellbeing flow, with the purpose of achieving shared objectives while simultaneously supporting individuals.

The way in which those people and **Relationships** are organized through different structures, and the nature of those structures, can have a monumental impact on the effectiveness of the communities in achieving their **Purpose** as well as the experience of the individuals working within them.

Prior to the Industrial Revolution, our

agriculturally based societies and communities followed a more natural rhythm and structure, as observed by Capra and Luisi in *The Systems View of Life*.[20] This was superseded by the steam age and the machine age, where factories, cities and offices became the new backdrops for organizing systems of work.

A combination of Frederick Taylor's scientific management theory with Max Weber's bureaucracy theory, both of which emerged in the industrial age, could be seen to have laid the foundations for the strict management of people with the intention of tightly controlling their output for maximum productivity, combined with a perceived importance of hierarchical structures.[149]

As we saw in 'What is the Nature of Work?', this is one of the enduring legacies we've inherited from the industrial era. While a hierarchical structure can have its benefits for the organization of work, and every organization ultimately has some level of hierarchy, it is when that structure is infused with rigidity, a lack of feedback loops, and unequal power-driven relationships, that the experience of work becomes one where people lose autonomy and trust. Hierarchy combined with a 'command and control' management approach can lead to harmful power distances between those doing the work and those managing the workers.

The organization becomes incapable of adapting and responding in order to survive and be resilient. In effect, it is when the social structures through which organizations function act mechanistically rather than as a living system that an organization's **Health** deteriorates and its resilience comes under **Threat**.

In order to remain competitive and meet the future expectations of customers, global banking group **ING** introduced agile ways of working in 2015 across its headquarters in the Netherlands. Inspired by working patterns at large technology companies, ING reorganized most of its staff into a series of small multidisciplinary squads of not more than nine people, each belonging to 'tribes' of around 150 people. Each tribe has a common or connected mission. Squads have considerable autonomy and are also flexible, so can change as organizational missions evolve; they are disbanded when a mission is complete. Other roles and structures, such as agile coaches and knowledge-focused 'chapters', help to underpin the successful execution of the structure.

This reorganization has been critical for the success of more agile working, removing the silos and barriers ING was experiencing, caused by the former traditional structure. ING Netherland's COO at the time, **Bart Schlatmann**, also reports on the importance of culture in making it happen, commenting: 'We have spent an enormous amount of energy and leadership time trying to role model the sort of behaviour – ownership, empowerment, customer centricity – that is appropriate in an agile culture.'

While transforming to such a radical model has had its challenges, ING reports a quicker time to market for products, increased employee engagement, smoother 'handovers' between different teams in terms of processes, and an overall better experience for customers.[150]

This Nature of Work view means that networks and structures of **Relationships** are intrinsic to how work gets done. The organization as its own living system within the wider ecosystem of work can help provide adaptive, flexible structures to group those relationships together in different ways in response to emergent needs and purposes, as new information is obtained and knowledge created both inside and outside the boundaries of the organization.

Organizing people, their **Relationships**, roles and the work to be done through flexible, agile, emergent structures doesn't mean anarchy (which is the absence of structure). Rather, it means allowing malleable constraints which flex and adapt over time in response to constant monitoring and assessment of the environment, within which autonomy, creativity and collaboration can be focused around a shared **Purpose**.

The way in which an organization is structured is therefore ultimately the cumulative effect of the many systems by which its network of people and their **Relationships** are grouped together. The nature of those structures, comprised of relationships and the **Biodiversity** of the organization, driven by its **Purpose** and **Roots**, and influenced and enabled by the different **Habitats** it creates, influence how quickly or slowly an organization is able to respond to new information, how it learns, and how it shares knowledge.

Large flock (murmuration) of starlings, Geldermalsen, the Netherlands. During January and February, hundreds of thousands of starlings gather in huge clouds. The power and agility of a seemingly self-organizing community has great potential for organizations.

Masai Mara, Kenya: three lionesses from the same pride, showing clear structure and purpose.

Adaptive organizational structures

A common trait of all effective social structures within living systems is, therefore, that they are adaptive.

Adaptive structures that enable the organization as a living, dynamic system rather than hindering it, have characteristics such as:

- shared and articulated objectives and goals that help set 'constraints' around the **Purpose** of the people being brought together, and that can be adapted as needed once new incoming information is processed
- clear roles and responsibilities, which can likewise evolve over time as needed, and bring together a diverse community of people based on their strengths and experience to help achieve the objectives
- open, clear and inclusive communication, which supports the different communication styles of the people involved
- constant feedback loops that exist over different timescales and at different levels, which support the filtering and processing of 'signals' about **Threats** and opportunities that relate to the group's **Purpose**, and help it to understand whether it's being successful
- cultures supportive of effective collaboration, including different learning and collaboration styles
- allowing for quick, localized decision-making within the larger framework of the organization
- the concept of **Life cycles** to help guide the adaptability of the structure, how long it needs to be in place, and how it overlaps with other structures that bring together groups of people.

The types of structure that work best for the task at hand will vary depending on the nature of the people being brought together and their **Purpose**; a structure that works for a one-off project focused on designing a new product, for example, may not be the correct structure for an ongoing public service provided to citizens.

Haier is a leading global manufacturer of white goods. Headquartered in China with over 70,000 employees, the company has radically evolved its structure over the past 35 years leading to great commercial success. The company's CEO, **Zhang Ruimin**, is admired as an innovative and influential thought leader in the management space, having led the company through five distinct transformations or regenerations, each of which builds on the last. The latest has been to evolve Haier into a truly networked company with a strong entrepreneurial streak and a relentless focus on customers.

This has been achieved by more or less eliminating middle management and organizing the company into an ecosystem of micro-enterprises, with 200 customer-focused enterprises and a far greater number dedicated to support and service. Enterprises have the power to make their own decisions, work closely with customers, employ who they like and get shares of profits.[151]

Zhang Ruimin's philosophy is known as **RenDanHeYi**. He comments: 'With the RenDanHeYi model we truly enter the network age... It's now time for every employee to be his or her own boss... So, with the RenDanHeYi model we move away from being like an empire (with a traditional, closed pyramid) to be more like a rain forest (with an open networked platform). Every empire will eventually collapse. A rain forest, on the other hand, can be sustained.'[152]

Haier is also involved in other innovative structures that support a more networked approach. Through Haier's subsidiary GE Appliances, the company has set up **FirstBuild**, a company that helps co-create home appliances and take them to market by working in partnership with a community of inventors, designers and entrepreneurs.[153]

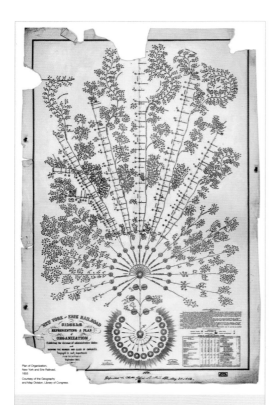

A copy of the first known documented organizational structure, from 1855, where the organization was depicted as a tree.[154]

Examples of different adaptive structures from which to draw inspiration are many and varied. Agile teams with squads, scrum masters and coaches in particular reflect the experiments happening in how work is structured, with the goal of encouraging more responsive ways of working.

Within both *Bioteams*[28] and *Nature of Business*[10], stories about swarms, colonies and superorganisms are drawn upon to better understand how nature has evolved its self-organizing, agile structures that can be applied to organizations. *Bioteams* also sets out a full methodology and framework, based on biomimicry, for creating different types of agile teams.

McKinsey too has drawn inspiration from nature to create a vision of how organizations need to function better, using the structure of a biological organism to illustrate its findings that more adaptive, flexible, agile organizations are performing better across organizational **Health** indicators.[154]

It found that 70% of agile organizations – categorized as having both high speed and robust stability – ranked in their top quartile of organizational **Health**, while those classed as 'bureaucratic' (slow and stable) or 'trapped' (slow and unstable) were both predominantly in the bottom and third quartiles of organizational health.[155] A clear shared **Purpose** and a network of empowered teams were found to be two of five clear hallmarks of an agile organization, with rapid decision and learning cycles; dynamic and cohesive communities; and enabling technology the other three.[156]

The Holocracy movement is another that has focused on how organizations can support localized self-organization around a shared **Purpose** and within shared constraints. **Zappos** has long been held as an example of an organization seeking to work in this way, albeit with its own mutations from the pure Holocracy framework.[157]

In some cases, organizations have even created new structures in the form of start-ups within the wider structure of the organization, acting with more autonomy and more nimbly than the larger surrounding structure is able to.

What is key is that organizations find the best blend of adaptive structures that helps their diverse network of people, combined with supportive, empathetic, empowering **Relationships**, to organize around achieving the organization's shared **Purpose**.

Emergent leadership for adaptive structures

This isn't to say that hierarchy isn't valuable and doesn't have its **Purpose**. We can see in nature, for example, how wolf packs have a leader, or observe the hierarchies in chimpanzee troops. Even within a self-organizing school of fish there are individuals that 'lead'. It is, as mentioned earlier, when these hierarchies are adopted with the rigid, mechanistic, industrialized mindset rather than a dynamic, adaptive living system one that the structure lacks resiliency and good **Health**.

Having a diverse and more fluid group of people who are able to take on leadership roles when required, and who work together to help

The world's first known documented version of an organizational chart (*see opposite*) dates back to 1855 in an image depicting the **New York and Erie Railroad** designed by **Daniel McCallum**. Rather than the strict hierarchical pyramids that had become popularized, McCallum visualized the organization structured as an emergent tree. The board of directors was seen as the roots, the chief officers as the trunk and the railroad's divisions and departments as the branches. The visualization decentralized decision-making into the localized 'branches', where the people working day to day on the frontline had access to the best and most up-to-date data, while still enabling knowledge flow and sharing back down into the 'roots' of the organization.[154]

Liberty Mutual Insurance is a global financial services company based in the US. When it created a highly innovative personalized digital assistant for employees that was integrated into its intranet, it started to get considerable interest from other organizations keen to implement a similar solution. Sensing a real opportunity, Liberty Mutual created **Workgrid**, a separate company but still owned by them, to evolve the digital assistant solution as a commercial offering.[158] The business operates very much like a start-up from within, and serves Liberty Mutual as a client. Workgrid continues to evolve its product offerings and has won several awards.[159]

Even highly competitive commercial rivals can collaborate and work together, although there are usually strict competition protocols required. In the UK, mobile telecommunications operators **Telefonica** (operating as O2) and **Vodafone** have shared mobile network resources for a number of years, principally through the creation of a joint venture company, **Cornerstone Telecommunications Infrastructure Ltd** (**CTIL**), in 2012. Both companies own half of CTIL.[160] The agreement from both parties has extended to the deployment of the 5G network.[161]

articulate **Purpose** and direction, is invaluable. Who 'takes the lead' at any one time may change depending on the challenge at hand – perhaps it will be a subject matter expert for one project but somebody deeply embedded in the frontline for the next.

Enabling this 'servant leader' mentality, where people know when to step back and listen, or when to step forward and lead, is integral to these living, dynamic structures of work.

And so, adaptive structures don't mean the end of hierarchy, simply a different conception of how hierarchy operates more fluidly around emergent leaders and objectives.

Organizations that are fearful of the impact of a wholesale restructure on performance and employee wellbeing in the short term can start to experiment with more fluid, agile approaches to organizing and structuring people.

The organization as a living system ultimately comprises a network of **Relationships** between people, a network that is constantly changing as people **Migrate** in, out and around the organization. Adaptive structures help that network of people to cluster together around emergent objectives and leaders, and to focus on what they can achieve together. Those structures have their own **Life cycle**, meaning they can evolve and adapt and die out as needed. Some may only exist for a matter of days, or hours. Others may last for the full life cycle of the organization itself.

The Unilever Foundry is a branded innovation initiative to attract start-ups, designers, inventors and entrepreneurs to collaborate with Unilever's brands. It aims to create strategic partnerships for the future and covers pitches, mentoring and investment. The Foundry offers a mentoring programme, a pilot programme to set up specific projects in partnership with Unilever, and occasional opportunities for investment from Unilever Ventures, the company's in-house venture capital set-up. To date, the programme has established more than 200 pilots with investment of over $20 million. The programme has also established co-working spaces in Singapore and Dublin to support collaboration between start-ups and Unilever.[162]

Sardines form a 'bait ball', Baja, California, providing group protection against predator sea marlins. By working with each other in a fluid, adaptive structure, the fish gain resilience.

Enabling inter-organization collaboration

An understanding of different dynamic, emergent structures can also help create cross-organizational relationships, bringing together a diverse mix of organizations in a macro version of the living system, to help solve the complex and 'wicked' problems we collectively face.

The Nature of Work as a living system means that organizations – as a defined community of people brought together under a shared **Purpose** – can themselves be structured in order to draw on different specialisms and pool resources to tackle more complex problems.

While mergers and acquisitions have long been sought for a variety of commercial reasons, what we're increasingly seeing are alliances, partnerships and collectives, where different organizations temporarily come together to collaborate and cooperate around innovative or emergent solutions and services to solve both immediate and longer-term challenges.

The COVID-19 pandemic, as a shared threat with monumental global and local impacts on the human species, served as a catalyst that demonstrated just how powerful enabling, emergent structures can be as a way of combining expertise and resources. Crowdsourced innovation pools, collectives and partnerships all emerged as ways of quickly responding to the new **Threats** and needs the pandemic created, such as the need to scale testing, personal protective equipment, public health campaigns, supply chains, welfare support, and more.[163]

Driven by more socially aware **Purposes**, organizations have the opportunity to frame a wider network of **Relationships**, identifying new groupings and structures that enable collaboration on a much larger scale. By focusing on the wider ecosystem and its needs, greater things can be achieved that benefit all.

Ask yourself

- What type of leader are you, or could you be? And in what sort of structure do you work best?
- Which structure metaphor from nature appeals most to you when you think about living systems of work – and why?
- Would the specific teams and structures in which you currently work best be described as a machine or a living system? How does this impact how effectively you and your colleagues are able to work together?
- How does your structure impact the speed with which you and your colleagues are able to respond to emergent threats and needs?
- Are there places in your organization and work community where more adaptive structures are in place? What is the impact of this?

- What are the different types of leadership that exist within your organization and work community and how do these impact – and how are they impacted by – the structures being used?
- Are there any structures that have enabled people in your organization and work community to collaborate closely with other organizations?
- Have you ever participated in any adaptive structures outside of work that were particularly effective, for example, through hobbies, professional networks or volunteering? What lessons could you take from those experiences and apply to how people structure themselves in your organization and work community?

Life cycles

How do organizations evolve over time?

Nature: The description given to the series of changes natural elements go through during their life span, from inception to end

Work: The phases of life in an organization as it evolves over time

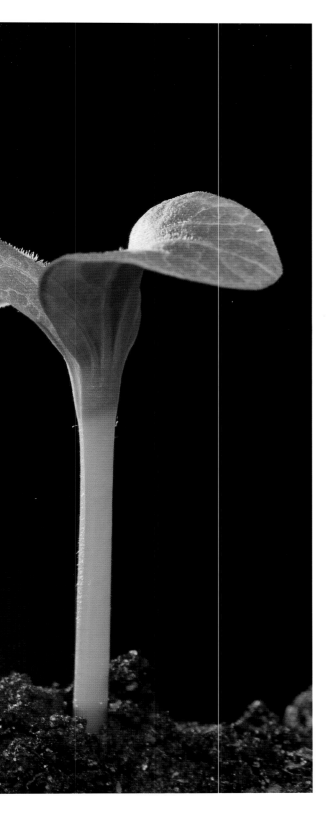

The reimagining of Nokia

Finnish company **Nokia** (best known for its mobile phones) was actually founded in 1865 as a paper mill operation near Tampere, with a second mill opened near the town of Nokia on the Nokianvirta River a couple of years later. It evolved first as an electricity generator, before then moving into rubber production. Through acquisition and near bankruptcy after the First World War, Nokia became involved in telecommunications, which led eventually to its pioneering role in mobile and then smart phones.[164] The arrival of the Apple iPhone was a blow to its dominance, from which it has not fully recovered, and a myriad range of acquisitions and divestments have marked its time since it was acquired by Microsoft in 2014.

What is striking about the Nokia story is the variety of sectors, services and restructuring it has been through. It reflects a company that might not always be on an upward commercial trajectory but clearly has the ability to adapt, innovate and step into entirely new markets. There is a freedom and creativity in the as-yet incomplete life cycle of this piece of fascinating corporate Finnish folklore.

The Nokia journey is one that has unfolded across many life cycles and is unusual in its range of activities. Nokia is in some ways more in line with the natural world than it might realize.

All has a beginning, all has an ending

Across Earth, indeed across the Universe, a cycle of life is unfolding constantly. In deserts, forests, oceans, towns, cities, villages, planets and stars, all is in motion. There is constant activity: new life, new growth, old life, decay, death, and again new life.

From a single hair on our bodies to the Sun itself, everything has a natural life span, starting from when and how it comes into being and ending after a certain passage of time. For some, that endpoint comes prematurely. Others far exceed their expected life span.

We delight at the arrival of lambs, chicks and calves, marvelling at the new life. As animals grow, if they survive, they will reach various milestones: mastering flight, first successful solo hunt, the age when mating becomes possible, then no longer is – and so on. They learn and pass on survival knowledge and skills, or instinctively know what's needed for survival.

And then, as time moves on, whether through ill health, a lack of essential resources, the predator–prey dynamic, or a whole host of other reasons, life comes to an end. As the body transitions into its next phase, re-entering nature to transform into different nutrients, for many species, that death will cause pain for those left behind. This is a phenomenon felt across the natural world, with elephants, magpies, otters, guinea pigs and many other animals having been found to grieve the loss of those with whom they have had close bonds (*see p.101*).

While many types of animal appear to recognize the death of one of their own kind, how they respond to this can vary widely, with highly divergent levels of emotionality and pragmatism played out. Some primates, for example, display signs of grieving, with cases of junior chimpanzees showing obvious grief when their mothers die. However, lions have been known to feed on the corpses of other lions if the meat is fresh enough. Naked mole rats when detecting another dead rat will drag the corpse to the existing latrine inside their tunnel system, fill the latrine, and then build another one, behaviour which is assumed to be driven by hygiene.[165]

Life cycles also aren't just exclusive to creatures. There is new growth in vegetation, as seedlings sprout and grow, then live in **Relationship** with their environment, before eventually dying and decaying, helping to feed a new cycle of life. There are periods of stagnancy and others of **Regeneration**.

All is naturally in balance – but when humans act without thinking about the implications of life cycles, this is how pollution and the accumulation of rubbish become forces of disruption in nature. If we fail to consider how things come into being and how they cease in order to return to nature, then we end up with harmful resource extraction and disposal practices, leading to ravaged landscapes and islands of plastic within our seas.[166]

Within larger structures, such as **Habitats** and entire ecosystems, life cycles unfold on a much grander scale. And yet, they still have their life span: their beginning, middle and end. In particular, four distinct phases of an ecosystem's life cycle have been identified: growth; conservation; collapse or release; and reorganization (which in turn leads to regrowth).[10] With the onset of the climate crisis, many of those life cycles are being cut short, with devastating consequences for those that rely on them for their own survival.

The entire living system of nature is thus in motion in every moment, with cells, organisms, social groupings, ecosystems, all on their own trajectories, overlapping and interacting with others. Every second, life cycles begin and life cycles end.

The work life cycle

Across the human species, our understanding of the life cycle is revealed partly in the many different ways we mark various transitional periods of our lives with rites of passage. Depending on the traditions of each culture, these can include ceremonies to celebrate or commemorate births, puberty, marriage, becoming a parent, menopause, retirement, death, and many more. Some transitions are biological. Others are social. Not everyone will experience every recognized life cycle event, whether through choice or not – or they may experience them at different stages of the life span.

B&Q, a DIY retailer in Britain, started a now fairly common trend when it deliberately set out to employ older and even retired workers, to provide the social benefit of work for an ageing population but also to give customers access to a range of staff that would reflect their own demographics. And, of course, the older workers have an acquired wealth of knowledge in the DIY field.[167]

At **DWG** a number of team members adopt a 'portfolio career' and combine their work in the digital workplace area with other completely unrelated careers in theatre production, marine tourism, academia, insurance sales, fiction writing, running yoga retreats or mindfulness coaching. These provide not only sources of income, but also fulfilling and rewarding opportunities for those involved.

"Life cycles aren't just exclusive to creatures."

Everything has a life cycle, but the natural 'decay' phase is too often not considered in human-made items. Better understanding of life cycles benefits both work and nature.

A group of elephants mourn a baby that has died recently. The mother and other elephants gently touch the body with their feet and trunks. Organizations and teams gain depth by respecting losses and suffering.

Our understanding of the ending of life cycles in particular manifests in a diverse number of ways. In cultures where ancestor veneration and remembrance are practised and celebrated, such as in Japan, Bali, some Native American tribes and Mexico, death is a passage into the next phase of a life cycle that extends beyond the passing of the body.[168]

Beliefs about the afterlife and souls, our **Relationship** with our ancestors and with future generations when we become ancestors ourselves, attitudes towards people in the winters of their life, plus fear of our own mortality, are all intimately connected with our understanding of the life cycle and how it unfolds. This impacts to what extent we are able to foresee and plan for the future and for endings – and to what degree we accept or fear them.

The ability, or inability, to work plays a key role in our own life cycles as humans. Whether children are forced to work through economic circumstances, whether someone is able to work as an adult, and the point when one finishes working through retirement, all have an impact on quality of life, capability to participate in culture and leisure, as well as access to the fundamentals needed for survival and wellbeing.

As a society, we develop generalized beliefs about people's capability and motivation for work according to where they are in their life cycle. We tend to make assumptions based on whether they're fresh out of the education system as a young adult, at an age when people typically start a family, within the middle phase

of their life cycle, or coming to the end of it.

This tendency to attribute to all people of a particular age the same opinions can lead to stereotyping. A typical observation in the media is that Millennials are lazy, entitled and narcissistic, although many observers have pointed out that this generation just want many of the same things from work as other generations.[169]

How this plays out in the workplace

Such beliefs and assumptions about what stage someone is at in their life cycle can lead to ageism (discrimination based on beliefs about someone's age, such as making assumptions about their capability to learn or fitness for work).[170] Or it can lead to sexism (discrimination based on beliefs about someone's gender), which we see in cases where companies choose not to hire women of a certain age for fear of their becoming pregnant or wanting to start a family[171], or when people are or aren't supported through their menstrual cycles.[172]

How we feel about *why* we're working is also intimately tied in with our own sense of **Purpose** of what our lives are for and how we wish to spend them. The very concept of a career is rooted in the progression of the life cycle and the expectation that, as we mature in age and experience, the work we do will somehow reflect this progression.

This may mean a single career built up over a lifetime, in some cases (now quite unusual) spent entirely within just one organization or, more likely, across a range of organizations.

At **McDonald's**, which has a predominantly younger workforce, there are **educational opportunities** for staff. In the US, a high-profile initiative offers staff the chance to improve their English skills, get a high school diploma and receive assistance with college fees. An accompanying app helps staff to plan education options.[173] In the UK, managers can study for a degree in Business Management while working at McDonald's.[174]

One former **Vodafone** senior manager shared with Paul that after taking early retirement due to illness, he remained onboard as a long-term contractor to **mentor new hires** and particularly those being sent on international placements where guidance from those who have walked the same path is invaluable.

At **Duke Energy**, employees reaching significant tenure milestones, such as 20 years of service, are prominently celebrated on the homepage of the intranet in the 'Employee Connections' section, showing that the company values the contributions of longer-serving employees.[175]

"Every organization needs elders for the younger generations."

Or it may consist of a portfolio of many different types of job. For those seeking to change career, either voluntarily by changing the specialism or industry in which they work, or through finding themselves forced to do so, the prospect of starting a new life cycle of work can be exciting and exhilarating – but also daunting and unsettling.

When our life spans were shorter, work was a lifelong activity. It wasn't until the human life span began to increase that the concept of not working past a certain age emerged, starting with Otto von Bismarck in the late 19th century.[176] But even then, it wasn't uncommon to work until you died.

That said, issues relating to retirement aren't simple. While some yearn for retirement as a chance to put their working lives behind them, others see work as intimately tied to **Purpose** and life satisfaction. In addition, how a society treats its elders – in terms of healthcare, social support, financial provisions, stigma, inclusion, isolation – can lead to huge disparities in what life after paid work looks like.

In the mechanistic understanding of work, a career life cycle has a pre-set trajectory, with clear inputs and outputs. Your usefulness to the working world is tied to your productivity. As a result, your capability to work, or what you're able to contribute, can be perceived to diminish or be limited based on life cycle phases or events, such as age, parenthood, illness, caregiving, menopause, and so on.

In the Nature of Work mindset, where work is understood as a living system, there is instead room for the **Biodiversity** of including people from across the different phases of the human life cycle, whether directly within the work community and/or through **Relationships** that cross organizational boundaries.

Recurring themes in work for many years have been 'younger workforce expectations' and 'five generations in one workplace'. These challenges – keeping the younger group engaged, attracted and fully contributing, while also ensuring inclusion across all ages – have kept HR and leadership teams focused on resolving these questions.

Every organization needs elders for the younger generations, who in turn can reverse mentor their elders through their energy, ideas and ambitions, which can be exciting and stimulating for the elders, keeping them fresh and engaged.[124] These intergenerational **Relationships** foster stewardship for the betterment of the company.

Increasingly, HR functions and employee experience initiatives are focusing on the employee life cycle, all the way from recruitment and onboarding, through career progression, to offboarding and keeping alumni connected, ensuring strong support and systems around all these stages. For example, **Southwest Airlines** advanced a company-wide employee experience strategy that paid particular attention to the work 'moments that matter'.[177]

During the COVID-19 crisis, some companies were also mindful to support working parents who faced challenges around childcare due to the impact on schools and nurseries. For example, **PwC** offered opportunities for an extended sabbatical at 20% pay while also providing more support for back-up childcare, various tuition programmes and job sharing. At **Google**, the company extended its paid family leave policy by eight weeks.[178]

Organizations that deny death struggle to live fully

And what of the life cycle of **Structures** as well as people? The life cycle of teams and of the organization itself? We know from nature that ecosystems can be in different phases of their life cycle; that they can emerge and that they can cease to exist, based on any number of cumulative factors. Organizations as structures experience the same cycles.

When Arie de Geus published his book *The Living Company* in 1997, the average life span of a company was 40 years, with a few exceptions where a company spanned several centuries.[9] Studies have shown that in the 1920s, the average life span of an organization was around 67 years. In 2017, it was 14 years. For start-ups in the UK, around half don't make it beyond 5 years.[179]

The numbers vary slightly depending on which study you look at and which country they relate to, but the trend across all are the same. While the human life cycle may have been elongated as life spans increase, that of organizations is contracting.

While we know that death is a crucial part of any living system as it makes way for new life, the impact of the death of an organization or one of its **Structures** can be monumental. Just as the death of an ecosystem can wipe out the animals, creatures and life that depended on

it, people's livelihoods and communities can be devasted by the failure of an organization, both through unemployment and the loss of the services or products it produced.

At the other end of the life cycle, however, emergent organizations mean new work opportunities, new products, new services.

Within the middle phases, between birth and death, lie moments that can either lead to **Regeneration** or tip things the other way, towards decay.

Which way the pendulum swings can be affected by any number of factors, many dependent on the organization's **Relationship** with its environment and the opportunities and **Threats** that lie both inside and outside of its structural boundaries.

For de Geus: 'Companies die because their managers focus on the economic activity of producing goods and services, and they forget that their organisation's true nature is that of a community of humans.' His work at Shell found that there are four key characteristics that contribute to an organization's longevity. They are:

- Sensitive to their environment (they have strong **Relationships** with their environment).
- Cohesive with a strong sense of identity (a clear understanding of their **Purpose** and **Roots**).
- Tolerant (they understand the importance of **Biodiversity**, particularly in terms of emergent ideas and innovations).
- Conservative in financing (they work within the constraints of their resources).[9]

The photographic giant **Kodak** was for a long time unassailable in film stock sales – until it catastrophically failed to adapt to the arrival of digital photography. However, in the latest twist to this tale, its business switched in 2020 to producing generic drug ingredients, causing the price of its shares to soar 1500% at one point in the year. Interestingly, this remarkable resurgence resulted from Chairman **Jim Continenza** asking during the early days of the pandemic: 'What can we do that would be useful?'. The life cycle of Kodak clearly has new twists coming.[180]

Working and living for the long term

Disruption caused by developments in technology, in particular, have led to accelerated life cycles, not just for organizations but for their services and products as well. This has created a crucial need to innovate in order to more quickly anticipate and respond to the needs of both work communities and the external environment. As a result, organizations are increasingly looking at how more adaptive **Structures** and ways of working can reduce the amount of time it takes to create new ideas and then bring them to fruition.

While there are benefits to these tighter life cycles, such as being able to be more flexible and adaptive and resilient, there are also consequences, such as not having the time to fully engage with potential unintended impacts. These may, for example, be on democracy, the environment, **Relationships** or **Health**.

Shorter life cycles for innovation raise the question of how to embrace longer-term and broader thinking, extending the horizons beyond the next product release to include not only the impact of that product on the environment but also the overall **Health** of people, communities and society.

There is a need to balance the survival of the living system of work in the short term through fast responses and survival in the long term by being able to recognize where an organization is in its life cycle, and how that can inform what should happen next.

The global COVID-19 pandemic has wrought devastation to the life cycle of many organizations, finding that their workforce, services, products, customers and clients have all been severely impacted, in turn causing either huge loss and pain, or in some cases accelerated growth due to increased demand.[181] The monumental loss of jobs is viewed by many as one answer to prolonging the life span of the organization, while others are also rethinking their **Purpose**.

Where is your organization in its life cycle?

Viewing the organization as a living system allows its life cycle to be perceived as fluid, transitional and ever-changing. Being able to understand where different parts of the organization are in their life cycle – and where the organization as a whole is – can help in planning for where new **Structures** and growth are needed, or others should be allowed to die in service of the organization's **Purpose**.

The aforementioned phases of an ecosystem's life cycle, in particular, can be helpful as a way of visualizing and mapping the life of organizational **Structures** (growth; conservation; collapse or release; and reorganization, from which there can be renewed growth). It's natural for different parts of an organization to be at differing phases of their life cycles; indeed, this can be a sign of a healthy living system. The question is whether life cycles as a narrative are actively being used to help uncover insights and inform decision-making. Where is birth happening or needed? Which parts, regions, sectors or services need nurturing so they can flourish?

At Moscow **Domodedovo Airport**, innovation is driven through a **crowdsourcing platform** and **knowledge management framework** that gathers, evaluates and rewards ideas from employees. With high-level backing from senior management and a mature approach driven by the KM function, the scheme has resulted in various high-impact innovations, including a restaurant on the roof of one of the terminal buildings, an on-site infant school for children of employees, the use of spare terminal space for exhibitions for passengers, and Segways for staff to travel between terminals.[182]

In the US, the **Hershey Chocolate Company** has continued on a path of **digital transformation and innovation**, deriving and continually refreshing a digital strategy, while investing significantly in areas such as big data. This has helped to improve efficiency in the manufacturing process and logistics. The company has also invested in its digital workplace and related digital employee experience.[183]

In the UK, where many high street retail chains are under threat, **John Lewis Partnership**'s chairman, **Dame Sharon White**, is working to understand where the organization is in its life cycle, and how its life span can be prolonged. Several department stores in the chain have been closed, but Dame Sharon is considering taking additional unconventional approaches to reinvigorate the largest employee-owned business in the UK. Founded in 1864, the company has already had a long life span and been through many 'cycles'. The next looks like it may expand into private and affordable housing, office space, an increased online presence and areas popular with employees such as gardening.[184]

Jack O'Lantern (*Omphalotus olearius*) fungi grow on tree trunks, consuming the wood and playing a significant role in nutrient cycling and carbon dioxide production as part of the forest life cycle. Organizations can evolve by allowing what is decaying to provide fertile ground for innovation.

Where is there decay, and does that matter, or is it inevitable? And which elements in the living system of your organization are dying?

We have all been to restaurants, hotels, retailers or fitness centres that we can instantly see are dying – and when we learn months or even years later that this has been their fate, we are not that surprised. Equally, we can sense (even at the idea stage) those services and venues that, when they arrive, are going to have the fresh energy to provide a healthy future. There are organizations that seem to keep regenerating and reimagining themselves over decades or longer, moving through the life cycle of ecosystems and extending their life span.

All things eventually come to an end in nature though – both organisms and the **Structures** through which their **Relationships** are organized. They each have their natural life cycle and life span over which that cycle unfolds.

Within the living system of work, we can apply this same understanding of life cycles to both humans and **Structures**. We can consider how we approach the human life cycle and all its various biological and social elements to better integrate and support it with and through work, as desires and needs and **Purpose** shift and evolve over a lifetime.

And we can consider how we approach and understand the **Structures** that make work possible. The language of life cycles can help us identify the **Threats** that put the life spans of organizations at risk. But it can also help us to understand if a structure is approaching its natural transition into the phase of decay or collapse, to consider which rites of passage we can create in order to prepare for that transition, and to look at whether within that transition we can also find opportunities for **Regeneration**.

Ask yourself

- Where are you in your own life cycle? How does this impact your work? And how well supported are you?
- Where are your close colleagues in their life cycles?
- Which age group is held in the highest esteem within your organization or work community? How can you all better recognize the value and wisdom to be found across the generations?
- Is there any discrimination, or assumptions made, based on where people are – or are thought to be – in their own life cycles within your organization or work community?
- How are people in your organization supported through the life cycle of their time there? Are some employee life cycle stages revered more than others?
- Where is your organization in its own life cycle, and are your leaders aware of it?
- Are different parts of your organization at different stages in their life cycle, such as different services and brands, and if so which stages? How well is this recognized and spoken about?
- How do people in your organization or work community treat the organizational life cycle stages of birth, growth, death and regeneration? Are there any collective rites of passage followed to mark each transitional phase?

Migration

Which people are attracted to your company, who is there for the longer term and who is just passing through?

Nature: The movement of creatures from one region to another, often prompted by seasonal or life cycle shifts, or threatening changes in habitat

Work: The movement of people between and within organizations, with each staying for different lengths of time

Wildebeest migration, Serengeti National Park, Tanzania. Modern organizations increasingly have a workforce that is highly mobile in a variety of ways.

Work is always moving

The **National Theatre** on London's Southbank has for decades been an artistic venue that forms one limb in a body of performance, music and art centres, the quality of which is respected around the world. Each venue within this half-mile strip of dense artistic experience has its own workforce and together they all exist as part of one larger organism.

Within the National, those working there vary in role and **Relationship**. There are permanent staff who work in administrative and artistic roles throughout the whole year, for whom this powerful Brutalist building is their enduring home. On any performance night there will also be actors, stage crew and front-of-house people, who may be attached to just a single play or a series in repertoire, their tenure at the National dependent on that season's schedule. And finally there may be volunteers, who appear on certain days throughout the year, as well as performers, musicians and exhibiting artists in the lobby, who might be there for a few days or nights only, before moving on to another venue.

While a supermarket chain may have a less widely varied workforce, it will nevertheless share some characteristics with the National: weekend workers, seasonal staff, employees on rotation, summer interns, gig economy people connected through distribution chains. In each organization, we find workers who live in the 'forest', others who migrate for periods of the year, and those who pass through depending on the season and conditions. Organizations have a flow of people for whom the forest will be home all the time; some of the time; or seldom. Migration can be found across this ecology of work and the more we see people as part of this natural system, the better we can adapt and enable growth in new and expansive ways, in tune with the flow of work and our lives.

Migration as cyclical and as a warning

Every evening, once the Sun has descended below the horizon and dusk has begun, a nocturnal migration begins across our oceans. From the depths of the water, all manner of plankton, fish and squid ascend to the surface to feed in safety, shielded from prey by the darkness of night.

Then, as dawn arrives, the movement back to the lower levels of the water where sunlight is less able to penetrate the density of water takes place.

Known as 'diurnal vertical migrations'[185], this daily mass movement is merely one example of how migration occurs across our natural world, with some journeys short and frequent, others lasting longer, and some only once in a lifetime.

"The impact of the climate crisis means that roughly half of all known species are gradually having to migrate to different habitats for survival."

Driven by regular phenomena such as seasonal changes to the temperature, breeding and feeding patterns, all manner of creatures have been found to be capable of navigating across immense distances together. At any one time, there are masses of creatures on the move across our globe, journeys that form a key part of their **Life cycle**.

Forests themselves are crucial to the migratory patterns of many different species of bird, with it estimated that between a quarter to a third of migrating birds depend on forests at one point or another during their life cycle.[186] A number of North America's songbirds, for example, such as the yellow warbler and the Tennessee warbler, are reliant on the tropical rainforests of Latin America to escape the colder winter months. Reforestation efforts have been crucial to preserving such annual migratory paths.[187]

It is surprising to learn that even forests migrate. It has been found that during and since the last ice age, different species of trees and plants have made the move across land in response to gradual changes in climate.[188] In fact, the many different ways in which tree species have evolved their seed disposal techniques play a key role in how forests have been able to migrate, journeys that have unfolded over millennia. Trees that weren't native to certain lands have, in time, moved into new regions out of necessity for their survival.[189]

And so, migration can also be triggered – and affected – by emergent **Threats**. The impact of the climate crisis, with global temperatures rising, has been found to mean that roughly half of all known species are gradually having to migrate to different habitats for survival.[190]

A parallel loss of **Habitat** through human construction and farming practices is also impacting the migratory journeys of species, disrupting well-worn and in some cases centuries-old paths, through the removal of crucial 'stopover' points, the loss of the final migration destination[191], or the addition of physical human-made obstacles (*see p.118*).[192]

Migration plays a crucial role in the natural world, as creatures – and plants – respond to both the Earth's cycles and their own. It can play an intrinsic part in how they survive the seasons. And it can serve as a warning signal that all is not well.

Physical migration and the Nature of Work

Migration is an integral characteristic of the Nature of Work as a living system in terms of both the constant movement of people – between and within organizations, as well as geographically – and as a potential warning signal that there are **Threats** causing people to leave.

Migration has been a characteristic of our own species throughout our evolution, involving both 'push' and 'pull' factors. Theories around mass migrations as far back as 60,000 or even 120,000 years ago are debated by academics, with these large-scale movements thought to have been driven by environmental factors such as climate and food availability[193], drivers that remain relevant today as motives for migration.

There are many examples of huge migration journeys undertaken in nature. A subspecies of **monarch butterflies** travels an almost 4,000-mile round journey in their lifetime. Pods of **grey whales** undertake an annual migration of 10,000 to 14,000 miles in search of rich feeding grounds. A particular type of **dragonfly** takes multiple generations to complete its migratory cycle from Africa to India and back.[194]

Migrating monarch butterflies cling to leaves, Pismo Beach, California. Recurring human transitions and collective rites of passage can be observed in work settings too.

In any given year, the **number of migrants** is high. It is estimated that in 2019 there were approximately 272 million international migrants, around 3.5% of the world's population, with 74% of this group considered to be of 'working age' (between 20 and 64). The global number of refugees in 2018 was 25.9 million, of which 52% were under the age of 18.[195]

The story of **Cadbury** stretches back to 1824 in the UK. Expansion of the business in the 1870s led to the Cadbury family purchasing land in the countryside for a new factory site. Underpinned by their Quaker beliefs, the family were deep believers in social reform, and wished to create low-cost, healthy environments for their workforce as an alternative to city life. As a result, a village was developed in connection to the factory site, with open natural spaces, creating a new local ecosystem in which work and life were within easy distance of each other, and preventing the need for many to 'migrate' to cities for work.[196]

Other factors such as war, conflict and prejudice also give cause for mass migration, as people's homelands become inhospitable, forcing them to leave and seek safety and refuge elsewhere.

The decision to migrate has therefore been found to be impacted by any number of issues. At a macro level, political, social, economic, environmental and demographic factors all play a role. At the micro level, education, religion, marital status and personal attitudes to migration can all impact the final decision taken by an individual as to whether to go or to stay, as well as affecting whether that person is actually able to afford the move financially.[197]

Scarcity or availability of work in both the start points and destinations of migrants are critical factors in their decision-making as to whether to leave or not and also where they will head for. They also have to consider how well they may be welcomed once they arrive.

Historically, industrialization has led to work opportunities shifting from rural areas to urban centres, resulting in a gravitation towards cities in terms of where people live and work. More recently, globalization has led to a shift in the countries where industries like manufacturing can be found, often driven by how much or how little people are paid for their work.

In this we can observe physical migration for work as a signal of a **Threat** resulting from the dearth of opportunity in people's home areas, just as in the natural world many creatures are being forced to migrate as a result of the climate crisis, which is impacting their natural habitats.

Cyclical migrations for work

In other cases, physical migration for work is more cyclical. The move to a different region for work may be seasonal, prompted by the **Life cycle** of the industry, such as is the case in agriculture or tourism. Or the migratory pattern may be prompted by the nature of people's work requiring frequent travel across a country or around the globe, for meetings, projects and any number of other reasons. For some, such as the 'digital nomad' community, migration is a way to experience different cultures while not needing to be in any one place for work.

And then there is our equivalent of the daily migrations found in nature: the commute. On an individual and a mass level, there is a daily flow of people travelling from their homes to a place of work, and then back again.

Even with the onset of the COVID-19 pandemic, which saw more than 100 countries in either partial or full lockdown by the end of March 2020[198], there were still those commuting to work: first essential workers, such as in healthcare and supermarkets, and then, as economies started to open up, in broader retail, hospitality and an increasing number of offices, even while many continued to work from home.

Within the legacy mechanistic mindset of work, the **Relationship** between physical migration and the organization is purely a case of access to labour, with humans just another resource. Decision-making about where labour is drawn from and where work opportunities will be created are economic considerations for the

114

organization only. How can we best minimize our costs in terms of location and labour, in order to maximize our income and profits?

Within the Nature of Work mindset, however, there is room for both economic considerations and all the other factors related to migration. It can take into account how physical migration for work and the location of work opportunities will impact communities, people's quality of life, access to support networks, the environment, infrastructure, transport, as well as the organization itself.

Working from anywhere

Remote working is now a common option for many organizations and people. As a result, physical migrations, such as having to move frequently for work and commuting, may no longer be necessary for many – as long as they are properly supported to 'work from anywhere'. This potentially creates opportunities for a long-term redistribution of where people can choose to live, positively impacting local communities at a distance from urban centres, as well as presenting a way to increase the **Biodiversity** of organizations through extending the area from which they're able to recruit talent. Combined with thinking such as the '15 Minute City' concept, which advocates having all your needs within a 15-minute walk or bike ride of your home, there is a huge opportunity to replace long commutes with reinvigorated local high streets and residential areas.[199]

Where physical migration for work is either desirable or necessary, organizations can consider, for example, where they're physically located, what that means for commuting and local employment opportunities, and how they are integral parts of those local communities. People can be supported to consider and mitigate any negative environmental impacts * that result from migrations for work. And considerations can be made as to how people forced to migrate can be included in work opportunities.

Some technology organizations with large headquarters are, for example, choosing to invest in their local area to ensure there are viable commuting options for employees, as well as meeting other community-focused commitments. This is particularly the case where their presence in a community has led to steep increases in property and rental prices, and gentrification. For example, **Microsoft** has committed to investing $500 million in affordable housing and a range of other initiatives in the Seattle area near its Redmond campus; this includes lending $225 million at subsidized rates for middle-income housing in six nearby cities, as well as investing $250 million in low-income housing.[200] The impact of initiatives such as these have been questioned, particularly with regards to how affordable such housing is for local residents[201], and while there is clearly more work to be done to find a solution, it shows that this will need to be via 'co-design' collaborations that include groups such as residents, local councils and the companies themselves.

Other companies have made active commitments to supporting refugees. For example, in 2017, **Starbucks** announced it would employ 10,000 refugees across its stores by 2022.[202] **IKEA** has also been active in this area, providing 2,500 refugees with job training and opportunities to improve their language skills across 300 stores, and committing €100 million from the IKEA Foundation to support various programmes that help boost refugee income, enabling them to 'become more self-reliant'.[203]

Organizations as part of the living system of work play a critical role in physical migration, both as push and pull factors. The Nature of Work mindset helps people who make decisions that impact and benefit from physical migration to consider their role within that broader ecosystem.

Why people migrate to and from organizations

Many of the reasons why people physically migrate can also be relevant to their decisions to join or leave organizations: we can observe factors such as salary (economic), personal development (social), discrimination and inclusivity (political), and habitat (environmental) all play out as push and pull factors for the migration that happens across organizations, as well as within them, as people move to different roles and teams.

The number of years people stay with one organization on average does, of course, vary widely, depending on a whole host of factors, including gender, education and age band.

That said, the research tends to show that people globally 'migrate' between organizations over the course of their careers and lives.

In the US, the median life span of someone staying with one organization has been found to be around 4.6 years.[204] In the UK, the average is around 5 years.[205] The concept of 'lifetime employment' is one that has historically held cultural value in Japan, although in 2014 the average tenure was found to be around 12.1 years.[206]

What's more, evidence suggests that the 'job-hopping' so frequently associated with Millennials[207], was also true of previous generations in their early 20s, including the Baby Boomers.[208] Those further along in their **Life cycles**, however, are likely to stay with one organization longer, indicating that the length of time you spend with an employer tends to increase as you get older.

In terms of the impact of **Habitat**, the 2010s saw a boom in organizations attempting to establish workplaces that would attract those 'migrating' to new jobs. Through office design, benefits, flexible working arrangements and other tempting factors, organizations tried to build in elements that would encourage people to join them and then stay.

However, too often, those organizations would fail to address *all* the **Health** factors that impact whether someone chooses to stay or not. A failure to thoughtfully create an environment where **Biodiversity** can flourish, for example, would mean that those from marginalized groups still experienced prejudice and discrimination.

Alumni networks are one way organizations keep in touch with employees and can provide a significant source of talent. For example, at **Microsoft**, alumni are particularly important; it has been reported that up to 15% of Microsoft employees are re-hires, with many other ex-employees involved in the Microsoft partner network and ecosystem.[209]

Consequently, the company invests in a significant alumni programme with nearly 50,000 ex-employees spread over 50 countries. Unusually, Microsoft alumni pay a small annual membership fee, which helps to position the value of the network, encourages active use and also makes the programme more sustainable. Benefits include an extensive event programme, many of the same benefits and discounts already enjoyed by employees, an online community that supports networking, learning opportunities, family subscriptions to Microsoft 365, and more.[210]

Or a lack of thought as to how the organization's **Purpose** impacts the wider world could affect that organization's reputation, making people question whether they really wanted to work there.

How migration impacts the health of the organization

In the Nature of Work mindset, migration between organizations is a given and aids each organization's **Health** if those migratory patterns are 'cyclical' and aligned with how the organization supports each person's **Life cycle**. New people coming in can bring fresh, new ideas and perspectives, learnings from previous organizations, and experiences. People exiting the organization, whether to retire or move on to their next challenge, can leave behind legacies of knowledge, learning and impact, in effect becoming 'ancestors' that can still – through alumni networks – pass on useful knowledge.

The organization can be seen as a 'stopover' **Habitat** that attracts people at specific points during the course of their life to spend time there contributing their skills and experience to the organization's **Purpose**, while also learning and developing. When the time is right, they then move on to the next destination in their migratory work journey.

There are already organizations thinking in this way, who know that it's unlikely that many of the people who are with them now will be there for the entirety of their career, and that at some point they will leave. This means the organization

can plan through a number of strategies to support people to have as good an experience as possible, so as to be able to contribute the best of themselves however long their time in that particular work community may be.

This manifests in any number of ways, such as strong onboarding and offboarding programmes, knowledge management initiatives that help people to pass on their knowledge and experience to others, and even encouraging 'internal migration' to recruit from within the organization.[177]

Initiatives to drive internal talent mobility can also help drive career development and encourage 'migration' within a company. For example, US healthcare insurer and provider **Anthem** invested heavily in an internal recruitment and careers portal to surface and promote opportunities, supporting ambitious recruitment targets.[211]

At the **Coca-Cola Company**, an ideation and development platform – named 'CokeStarter' – helped crowdsource employee ideas and turn them into funded projects that then provided development opportunities for employees, not only solving company problems but also encouraging development and internal career progression.[182]

However, people can also experience involuntary migration when forced out of their organizations through, for example, redundancies or the decline of their company. The COVID-19 pandemic, in particular, saw mass – mostly reluctant – 'migrations' out of

In pre-COVID-19 days, at **Microsoft**, the 300-strong sales team based in New York was highly mobile every day – but returning to the company's downtown Manhattan base in Times Square could prove both inefficient and extremely inconvenient for team members, depending on where their work had taken them that day, or the distance from their home. To combat this, most of the team was given access to flexible workspace provider **WeWork**'s locations throughout New York, meaning they could choose to work from a variety of locations across Manhattan, Brooklyn and Queens. The results were reduced commuting times and a more satisfied and productive workforce.[212]

The daily migrations of hedgehogs are being adversely impacted by the human-built environment, and particularly by fences in gardens that they can't get through. Disruptions to normal migratory patterns in work can be a sign of threats that require vigilance.

Red crab migration, Christmas Island, Indian Ocean, 1,500km west of Australian mainland. The first rainfall of the year triggers millions of adult red crabs to make the journey from their normal forest habitat towards the beach to spawn.

organizations, as thousands upon thousands of people were made redundant, resulting in global increases in unemployment.

The impacts of such events can be traumatic for individuals, their families, communities and for organizations. The mechanistic mindset means approaching these situations as a mere calculation, while the Nature of Work mindset sees the full living system of work and how it intersects with people's lives, the **Health** and wellbeing of communities, and more. It asks: How can this person be supported as they now need to find their next destination?

In the wake of COVID-19, some organizations making redundancies have been trying to adopt this approach. For example, **Airbnb** moved part of its recruitment team into job placement positions to support people being made redundant in trying to find another role.[213]

Migration is an integral part of the living system of work, as people both physically move around for their work and also move between organizations over the course of their life. The questions are how can people make their organizations attractive to the right people needed for the job at hand, support them during their time there so they know they belong and are in the right place, and then help them as best they can as they move on to the next stage in their migratory journeys?

Ask yourself

- What migrations have you made throughout the course of your career, both physical and between different organizations or roles? What were the 'push' and 'pull' factors of those migrations?

- What physical migrations occur within your organization or work community through travel for work, and what is the impact of those migrations?

- Does your organization or work community have its own natural migratory patterns amongst its workforce, dependent on, for example, the season? If so, what does that look like?

- How long do people stay with your organization before they migrate, and does this vary according to where they are in their life cycle?

- What are the potential 'push' factors in your organization or work community that cause people to leave? Are there any signs of threats that are pushing people away?

- What are the potential 'pull' factors that cause people to join and to stay?

- Does the ecosystem of your organization or work community provide opportunities for people to grow and change their careers within it?

- How does your organization keep in touch with people who have left?

- And how does your organization approach hard decisions, such as redundancies? How could this be improved?

Threats

How to navigate the inevitable challenges and dangers your organization faces, externally and from within

Nature: An element, such as predator or loss of habitat, likely to cause damage or danger

Work: External or internal risks or dangers that can damage or even destroy an organization

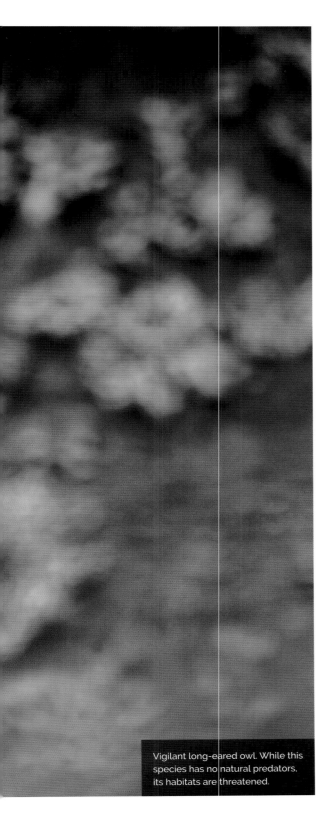

Vigilant long-eared owl. While this species has no natural predators, its habitats are threatened.

Predators, disease and destruction

It is appealing to present the 'organization as organism', from machine to living system, narrative as benign and even peaceful, endlessly at ease with itself. After all, breathing vitality and energy and **Health** into your company by experiencing your own ecology is liberating and (hopefully) inspiring.

But that is a partial and only selective reading of this new story of work. Every natural system lives constantly with a range of threats – predators, disease, destruction and unforeseen events. So, in case we relax into a beatific state, we need to understand where and how the living system of your organization can prepare for and address threats, which may arise not only in the external environment but from within too. In other cases, the organization itself may be the threat posed to others.

In William Shakespeare's timeless tragedy *King Lear*, the aging king of Britain decides to divide his kingdom evenly among his three daughters. First, he tests his daughters, asking each of them how much they love him. Goneril and Regan, his older daughters, give flattering answers. But Cordelia, Lear's youngest and favourite daughter, remains silent, implying that words cannot describe her love.

Lear disowns Cordelia, and she leaves instead for France, where the French king wants to marry her – against her father's wishes. Goneril and Regan undermine the little authority Lear still holds and, unable to live with their betrayal, the king slowly goes insane.

Suffice to say, the story ends badly for Lear and for his realm.

The tale of King Lear shows that dangers and threats we experience can arise when disease starts within and is allowed to fester – and in time it might just weaken an organization or render it obsolete.

It is a brave person who would challenge the seemingly unstoppable economic power of **Apple**, which at the time of writing was the first company to reach a valuation of $2 trillion[214] – but viewed through a living system lens, the market-turning innovations that were experienced time and again under the tenure of its co-founder Steve Jobs have all but disappeared. Yes, there are upgrades and attractive accessories, but there has been nothing since Jobs that has resulted in a whole new category of technology as the iPhone did when launched in 2007, or the iPad in 2010. There is a systemic weakness in Apple that has not yet been healed. Viewed as a living system, Apple's financial **Health** is clearly extraordinarily robust but its innovation health remains weak when compared with its historic strength in that critical area.

Vigilance in the face of threats

Threats to survival pervade the natural world, playing a crucial role in keeping our ecosystems in balance. Animals that are preyed upon need to be constantly on the lookout, continually monitoring their surroundings for signs of any predators. They develop biological and

In 2013, **HSBC** set up an ambitious 'employee listening programme' as part of a wider cultural shift to move away from an overreliance on top-down communication. The **Exchange** programme is centred around regular meetings that managers hold with their teams, where all the manager does is listen and act as a facilitator to encourage participation. There is no set agenda, so employees are free to give feedback, and managers do not respond or discuss the issues. After the meetings, the information gleaned is entered into an online portal, which then aggregates global data and identifies trends, insights and issues to inform and allow senior management to take any necessary actions. The initiative was rolled out globally through HSBC.[215]

behavioural adaptations to help them survive these immediate threats.

Such vigilance enables prey animals to spot the signals of danger early. If they are in a group, whether of just their own species or cross-species, the responsibility can be shared and the alarm instantly sounded to quickly communicate to the other group members the need to react. If they are alone, their energy will need to be carefully split between vigilance and other activities like foraging.

In the face of danger, some creatures will hide in plain sight, relying on the effectiveness of their natural camouflage to blend them into their habitat. Some will run, relying on their speed to escape. Others fight back, chasing off the predator – and then there are those who have developed 'bluff' behaviours and physical adaptations that make them seem larger than they really are in an effort to appear as a threat themselves (*see opposite*).

Working together can be the safest way

But threats don't just come from predators. For all manner of creatures and plants, there is competition for resources and threats from the elements and the environment itself. For many, cooperation and collaboration – or 'mutualism', as we saw in **Relationships** – are integral to addressing competition; a fight is risky for all, with its own threats of injury and death. Working together, on the other hand, can often benefit everyone, particularly when resources are plentiful.

For predators that hunt in groups, collaboration makes the likelihood of success greater, meaning that none go hungry. For prey that feed in groups, it can mean less attention needs to be given to being vigilant, releasing resources and energy that can be spent on looking for food. Cooperation can also mean that creatures – and plants such as trees – give each other enough space to access the nutrients and elements they need for survival, rather than being more densely packed together and in competition with each other in a smaller patch (*see p.128*).

Memory is crucial for remembering and learning what constitutes a threat. It's been found that plants 'remember' which previous threats have caused harm and which haven't, meaning they can react accordingly by either defending themselves or not (*see pp.147–148*). This helps them preserve crucial energy.[216]

Animals too have specialized memories that help them to recall past experiences, allowing them to react in the present and plan for the future.[217] This is how we see those cyclical **Migrations** happen, as different species move away from the threat of the changing seasons towards more welcoming **Habitats** based on individual and collective memories.

The natural world has evolved to create resilience in the face of threats at all its various levels, whether through the ways in which flora and fauna behave, or through the **Regeneration** that plays such a crucial role in both the survival of ecosystems and the self-healing of organisms.

There are a number of **animals who use deception** in order to protect themselves from threats. **Male green frogs**, native to North America, use their croaks to indicate to rival males their relative size. However, some frogs have been recorded lowering their croaks to make them sound bigger than they actually are.[218] Meanwhile, in the ocean, **cuttlefish** and some related species have males that can change colour and contract in size in order to appear as a female to protect themselves from larger males when fertilizing eggs. The **intelligence** of these males gets even more sophisticated as they can on one side appear female and on the other male. This allows them simultaneously to deal with the threat of competition, while continuing to court their potential mate.[219]

The chameleon is well known for being able to change its appearance to provide camouflage against threats.

Although the behavioural testing of animals such as rats in laboratory conditions has received criticism for not supporting the observation of natural behaviours – as well as for ethical reasons – studies of both domesticated and wild rats have shown them to have excellent **episodic and spatial memories**.[220] Their ability to remember where they've stored or previously found food, social behaviours such as 'favours' they've received from other rats in the past[221], and their tendency to ignore predator scents while foraging in familiar habitats[222] all help them to be vigilant and to assess potential threats to their survival.

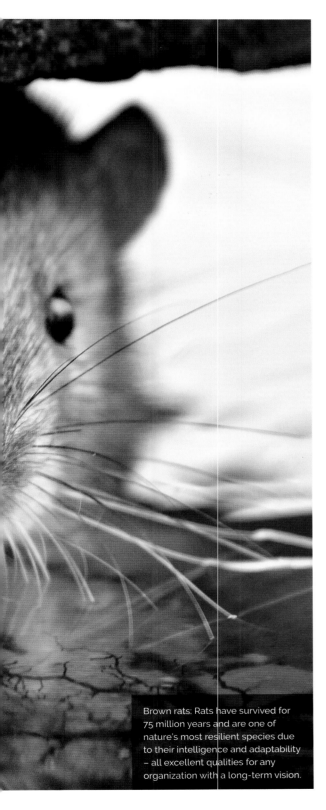

Brown rats: Rats have survived for 75 million years and are one of nature's most resilient species due to their intelligence and adaptability – all excellent qualities for any organization with a long-term vision.

And while threats are important in keeping nature in balance, it is when new threats emerge – such as the climate crisis or the human-built environment – that this resilience is tested in ways never before needed.

Where are you staying vigilant? What are you ignoring?

The world of work has, of course, always been subject to threats. The agrarian age suffered agricultural challenges in the form of adverse weather, pests and diseases. As the industrial age took hold, different kinds of threat emerged; for instance, long-distance supply chains might be affected when a ship was lost at sea with both its crew and goods. Later on, labour strikes increasingly became a factor.

The data and reports that people in an organization seek, as well as where budget is prioritized, can in turn reveal much about what they currently consider to be a threat and therefore need to be vigilant towards.

Historically, these perceived threats have most often been around the economics of an organization: the money coming in and going out. Financial key performance indicators (KPIs) and reporting have been emphasized as the main way of assessing the **Health** of an organization as, ultimately, this reflects the money needed to pay people's wages and purchase the tools and materials required to get work done. One way that organizations have often dealt with such financial threats has been with cost-cutting measures.

But, as we've moved into a living age, the threats facing organizations have morphed once again. Understanding the organization as part of a wider ecosystem enables more effective vigilance and improved resilience towards emergent threats on a more diverse range of horizons.

Some external threats, such as the climate crisis, COVID-19 pandemic, competition or technological disruption, are seemingly out of an organization's immediate sphere of influence. Other internal threats are more within its control.

Just as the animal and plant kingdoms are vigilant to all kinds of changes in and signals from their own environments and their **Health**, which may indicate a threat, so people within an organization need to understand and be vigilant to what can constitute a threat to their organization. These threats may be immediate, imminent or potential, and may manifest both inside the boundaries of the organization or within its wider environment.

Organizations are developing all sorts of frameworks, tools and reporting systems to help them identify potential and actual threats. Some of these have long histories, such as the SWOT analysis model, which asks people to consider strengths, weaknesses, opportunities and threats.[223] Others are a result of advances in technology that harness the ability to collect and analyse huge amounts of data in order to identify patterns taking place both within and outside the boundaries of the organization.

Taking on board learnings from the **Relationships** element of Nature of Work, where we considered the organization and its people in relation to its surrounding environment, a broader view can also be

126

HubSpot produces marketing sales and service software. In order to drive a customer-first culture at HubSpot, the company launched a global **Voice of the Customer (VoC)** program that aggregates customer feedback and metrics from approximately 40 channels across 20 different systems. The program delivers insights that allow customer-facing teams to respond quickly to customer needs and address any 'friction'.

Initiatives from the program include a regular metrics report, customer meetings with senior leaders that help drive empathy, and the creation of a customer advisory council. With customers' happiness central to HubSpot success, the program identifies any threats caused by customer dissatisfaction and issues, allowing HubSpot to take any necessary action to ensure customers experience great service.[224]

adopted, using methodologies such as the STEEPLE framework[225] or Doughnut economics model[135], to consider where potential threats lie within areas such as the social, technological, environmental, political and legal horizons.

Having a Nature of Work understanding of **Health**, too, can help people to be vigilant towards any internal threats that are manifesting based on where an organization is in terms of each of the Nature of Work elements. If its health is low in any one of these areas, this can constitute a threat that needs to be addressed.

Having the right people in place, who are able to recognize the threat signals being sent out, is crucial. As in the meerkat social groupings, who are the 'sentries' keeping an eye on the horizon and communicating back the alert signal to the group (*see pp.71–72*)? Do the sentries rotate and change? Are they diverse enough in their specialisms? Is the group learning together about new threats they haven't encountered before, while also sharing knowledge about old threats?

Creating resilience to threats

From an internal perspective, being able to monitor the **Health** of your organization across the 12 Nature of Work elements is an important way of helping the organization to bolster its resilience to threats.

If **Biodiversity** is low, **Relationships** aren't being identified and nurtured, **Structures** aren't adaptive or there is too high or low a level of **Migration**, for example, these are all signs of threats to the health of the organization that may impact its longevity and overall resilience

to external challenges. What's more, as we'll see in **Regeneration**, the ability to regrow from crisis is crucial.

Leading up to 2020, threats such as technological disruption had already prompted a strong focus on what's been termed the 'Future of Work', and how essential it is for organizations to adapt or otherwise die in the ever-increasingly complex world humans are creating. Resilience here meant the ability to survive, assessing how big a threat the organization was facing, and what it needed to do in order to **Regenerate**. Innovative **Structures**, such as through increased mergers and acquisitions, more agile approaches and new partnerships, emerged as ways to try and make sure technology-driven threats didn't overcome the organization.

However, then 2020 saw the human species face an immediate and global threat on a scale it hadn't before in living memory – and which potentially acts as a precursor to how, together, we will increasingly need to collaborate in the face of such profound existential threats as climate change. It showed many that the 'Future of Work' had arrived now – and, for us, it served to underline the urgency of adapting to a Nature of Work way of thinking.

The particular nature of the pandemic threat affected different organizations and industries in a spectrum of ways. Some that were already largely reliant on office-based workers and equipped with a strong digital workplace were able to adapt quickly as soon as staff were forced to work from home. However, the widescale sudden change in working conditions for many necessitated vigilance towards new

Stagecoach is a UK-based bus operating company that rolled out the Blink mobile solution to support and connect its frontline workforce as well as its office-based people. By putting reporting and communication tools into the hands of its drivers and those located in depots, a Managing Director commented that they had learnt more in two weeks of reading the comments on the platform about their services in and around one of their cities than he could ever have learned by sitting in the canteen talking to the drivers for hours on end. Tools rolled out included drivers being able **to report a 'near miss' or 'accident'** from their phones, as well as specific feedback on the network and antisocial behaviour reports. The specific tools were supplemented with enterprise social network capability, supporting staff to share knowledge and information more easily.[226]

'Crown shyness' in trees: cooperation in nature means sharing and giving space, rather than competing for it, so that all are able to access resources.

Even the genteel world of **cricket** uses technology to assess threats. For example, the England cricket team has the ability to call up any video of any player in the first-class game on an iPad, to assess how best to compete against that player. A team analyst from the **Performance Analysis Team** travels with the touring cricket team and uses software to code every ball bowled; analysis from this then helps the team to prepare for the next day's play and for future matches.[227]

Wolves operating as a pack: working together is a common way for social animals to help each other to be vigilant to threats.

threats, such as the potential impact on people's mental health and wellbeing, or the impact on equity. Again, some organizations were able to adapt more quickly than others in the face of these new threats to their people.

Other industries that are more reliant on face-to-face relationships and interactions, such as hospitality[228], events[229], the arts[230], travel[231] and some areas of retail, faced much larger threats, finding themselves in some countries prevented from being able to serve their customers and confronted with massively reduced demand for their services and products. While some were able to adapt, such as restaurants who switched to delivery models or were able to serve their communities in different ways, others such as the travel industry were confronted with an existential threat to their very survival. For many, collaboration and cooperation became a way of increasing resilience, as we saw in **Purpose**.

For all, the very real **Health** threats associated with working through a pandemic are impacting areas such as **Habitats**, **Relationships** and **Life cycles**, as organizations and their people are forced to adapt both their working and personal lives.

As the working world comes to terms with living through a pandemic and with a new virus, the question of how resilient both people and organizations are to face down new threats is raised.

The power of **Relationships** between organizations to address complex, 'wicked' problems can be strong as long as those organizations are either already very healthy

With the onset of COVID-19, US-based utility company **Duke Energy** was able to respond exceptionally quickly, enabling around half of its workers (more than 20,000 employees) to work remotely, covering virtually every office-based role, including call centre staff. A project that would normally have taken many months to achieve was completed in days, thanks in large part to previous investments in collaboration software and other technology. The investment in the company's employee portal also meant the digital workplace team was able to set up a site very rapidly to provide authoritative employee communications and support resources. As well as the technology being a critical enabler for 'organizational readiness', Duke Energy's empathetic and 'can-do' culture enabled quick decisions that would keep employees safe and support customers.[232]

The elephant hawk-moth caterpillar is able to disguise itself as a snake in order to deter predators. In work, it's important to know your environment and recognize threats to be able to adapt and respond to them.

within themselves, or are able and willing to increase their mutual **Health** through partnerships. They need also to be self-aware enough to recognize if they themselves are the threat to the living system of work, and

when competition may be harmful to others or indeed to themselves. In that case, cooperation or collaboration may be the better way forward for all.

With huge potential threats such as the

climate crisis on the horizon for all of us – and new ones likely to emerge – we can collectively work together not only to create the necessary vigilance to alert one another but also the resilience to respond and, in time, regenerate.

Ask yourself

- Which threats are you and others in your organization or work community best attuned to, and how does this manifest itself? What are the different 'horizons' over space and time that are monitored for threats, both near and far?

- Who are the 'sentries' that most commonly report back on threats, and what tools, skills and knowledge do they use?

- Are the 'sentries' formed of a diverse group? If so, what are the benefits of that? Are there any people not currently a part of the group who could help broaden out the threats towards which the organization is vigilant?

- Do some parts of the organization value information about certain threats over others? What's the impact of this on the organization's ability to respond to threats?

- What are the different defence mechanisms that people in your organization or work community tend to adopt in the face of threats? What are the different impacts of each mechanism?

- Which potential threats are people in your organization or work community not vigilant towards that you can think of? How could this change?

- Are there any instances where your organization or work community itself could pose a threat, and if so what type?

- Are there any ways in which people cooperating and collaborating – rather than competing – could support your organization or work community to be more resilient to threats?

Regeneration

Renewal at many levels is at the heart of organizations that remain successful over time.

Nature: The renewal, restoration and growth that makes organisms and ecosystems resilient to natural fluctuations or events that cause disturbance or damage

Work: The ability to refresh, restore and innovate across many dimensions and over time

How far ahead is the future?

German car manufacturer **BMW** has a project called 'The Next 100 Years'.[233] The team working on this project talk very personally about their childhood experiences and formative influences – riding horses in Mexico, marvelling at the colour of the water in the Mediterranean Sea, and learning about design by playing with boxes in rural Denmark. By harnessing the creative and technical imaginations of designers from many walks of life and work, BMW is allowing itself the freedom to reimagine; the chance to regenerate itself for a world it cannot know with certainty but can at least intuit and then help fashion.

BMW has already been through multiple regenerations in its more than 100-year history, starting out in 1916 as a manufacturer of aircraft engines, then progressing to producing motorcycles, and today cars. Reaching the centenary point in its **Life cycle** served as a rite of passage to reflect on the organization's **Roots**, **Purpose** and potential **Threats**, as its people turned to consider what the next 100 years could bring.

Out of this, the people working on the BMW project put together six key hypotheses for the future of individual mobility, which together paint a picture of BMW's view of the future, from the imperative for organizations to take on responsibility for the environment and their people, to 'technology is becoming human'. Out of this, BMW seeks not just to maintain the status quo, but to regenerate, resulting in a far-reaching vision that has been shared publicly.[234]

BMW knows that its future lies beyond fossil fuels and is actively exploring what alternative energy might look like not just in 2050 but as far ahead as 2116. It recognizes, as we do, that so many parts of the Earth and our natural world have been damaged, degraded and rendered extinct. There is much repair, healing and regeneration needed, and it will take decades and probably centuries to fully restore and bring the Earth and ourselves back to the level of vitality and strength we know is possible. That is a challenge of daunting proportions for our living age. We may have woken up (albeit far later than we wish we had) to the scale of the tragedy but at least we are now ever more aware and awake.

As the story of work departs from its mechanistic phase to consider the organization as a living system, what becomes possible is not simply to remove the 'degraded' parts of the workplace but instead to be able to create the fertile ground for true innovation, creativity and imagination.

Trying to innovate within a collapsing system of mechanization and control, with unchecked resource depletion, becomes a weak and fragile process, leading to degradation and decay. Once we start to experience our work and colleagues, the interplay of humans and technologies, as actually alive, doors to new horizons open, allowing newly inspiring and surprising services, products and markets to come into view.

Trees in the Deadvlei (dead marsh) clay pan, Namibia, which died more than 600 years ago due to drought and successive years of dune formation. The dunes prevent water from reaching the clay pan even when occasional rain falls and the trunks persist because the wood does not decay in this dry environment. However, as an example of regeneration, some plant forms (the smaller shrubs and trees) have adapted to make the most of early morning mists that result from moist ocean winds crossing the dunes.

Tamworth pig on the Knepp Estate, England: Knepp is famous for its rewilding and regeneration approaches. Control is exchanged for natural growth, which provides greater diversity and richness in the environment.[235]

Isabella Tree and her husband **Charlie Burrell** have restored 3,500 acres of degraded land in West Sussex, England. Now, ponies, longhorn cattle, red deer and Tamworth pigs roam free across this formerly farmed land, showing what can be done to restore and regenerate. Isabella's book *Wilding* describes this project that is renewing the ecosystem after decades of intensive agriculture on their Knepp estate.[235]

The results have been spectacular; in what has become a glorious 'mess', the animals live out in the open all year round and give birth unassisted by humans. Formerly common plants, as well as some more rare ones, have returned in profusion, together with insects, bats and other organisms. Scrubland, wetland and other habitats are gradually renewing themselves as the herbicides and pesticides subside. The increase in the variety and abundance of birds has been particularly astonishing, with nightingales, peregrine falcons and turtle doves – all threatened species – returning.

What is revealed when damage to the Earth is healed is not just that it is brought back to a level of 'normality', but that it regenerates and brings with it unexpected benefits, and an entirely new and refreshed environment.

Nature as regenerative

Nature has the power to heal; to regenerate both in the aftermath of harm and destruction, and when opportunities to grow present themselves. We can also observe this capability in ourselves, as our skin heals itself after a cut or our bones reunite after a break. The axolotl, a type of salamander, goes one step further, being able to regenerate whole limbs or organs when these are damaged or lost (*see p.143*).[238]

But regeneration in nature goes beyond an individual organism's ability to heal. It goes to the heart of how whole ecosystems, such as forests, can survive for thousands of years, even as individual trees within them pass through their own **Life cycles**, either naturally or because they are felled by introduced **Threats**.

Certain forest systems, for example, have evolved to be able to regenerate in the aftermath of the naturally occurring threat of fire, a factor that has historically played a natural and important role in the **Life cycle** of forests. In the 21st century, however, as a result of both the climate crisis and human activity, fire has turned into a much more devastating and traumatic **Threat**.[239]

As safeguards against the more 'normal' cycles of fire, species such as the shortleaf pine produce buds that lie dormant underground within their root systems, ready to resprout whenever the trees above ground come under attack from burning. Others, such as the Jack pine (*see below*), have developed pinecones that can exist for years on the tree, their seeds

Brewdog, a Scottish craft brewery, is investing £30 million towards its goal of becoming carbon negative, removing double the amount of carbon it produces each year. The company has acquired 2,000 acres of land in the Scottish Highlands and plans to plant a million trees. Around three quarters of the land will be woodland, with the remainder restored peatlands.[236] The company is already carbon neutral, having invested £2 million in different offset initiatives as well as making various changes to its production methods; for example, leftover grain from the brewing process is turned into gas.[237]

Jack pine cone: the cone stays glued shut with resin, until extreme temperatures of fire melt the resin, releasing seeds and enabling the tree under threat to regenerate.

protected by a hard, thick outer shell glued tightly shut by resin. It is only in the heat of a fire that the resin will melt, meaning that, while the tree itself may not survive, its seeds become 'unlocked', ready to be carried away by the wind and gravity.[240] In the open spaces that fire leaves behind in its wake, new trees and life can take seed. The sun is able to reach parts of the forest that were previously impenetrable due to the shade of the former trees' canopy. Nutrients lying in the forest floor are freed.[241]

Life on Earth survives through regeneration in the face of **Threats**, either due to the individual's ability to heal or because the ecosystem persists when individual organisms die. Even in the face of decreasing **Biodiversity**, loss of **Habitats**, rising temperatures and all the many ways in which the climate crisis is manifesting, we can see glimmers of hope for a way forward. Both natural regeneration and our own decisions and actions to change human behaviour and practices will play crucial roles in creating space for and encouraging the healing of natural systems.

Rewilding initiatives rely on nature's ability to regenerate if given the right conditions to do so.[242] Species previously in decline or that have become extinct in their natural **Habitats** can sometimes be reintroduced and allowed to thrive. Beavers, for example, have been reintroduced in England after having been absent for 400 years, supported by evidence that they play a crucial role in ecosystem health (*see right*).[243] The findings in England have been mirrored by studies in North America: here, native beavers have historically played a crucial role in creating 'fireproof refuges' through their dam-building activity, which provides shelter for both animals and plants from wildfires. This research is helping to establish how beavers can play a key role in helping ecosystems to regenerate and regain resiliency towards fire.[244]

Forests and trees in particular are the focus of many regeneration initiatives. Strategic tree planting is a key activity in both helping critical **Habitats** to survive, and increasing the footprint of these 'lungs of the Earth' that help absorb excess carbon dioxide.

To heal is thus an intrinsic behaviour of nature. And not just to heal, but to grow back stronger.

Lu Ying, Founder of **Future Urban Living** and advocate for circular economies, highlights examples of organizations integrating the full life cycle of their products into their manufacturing processes, as a method of reshaping their purpose around creating better futures, such as:
- **General Motors**, which has an initiative that recycles and reuses its byproduct, generating $1 billion new revenue a year in addition to saving costs.
- **Caterpillar**, which has been able to save 40–50% of its production costs through remanufacturing.
- **MUD Jeans**, which creates jeans with an upcycle, client retention and subscription model.[245]

Young Eurasian beaver nibbling a willow twig in the River Otter, part of a reintroduction project by Devon Wildlife Trust, England. This is one of the first wild beavers to live on the river in 400 years.

Lego is a brand that has continued to regenerate, innovating and reinventing itself and its products. This approach has led some to hail the Lego story as 'the greatest turnaround in corporate history'. In 2003, the company was in trouble, with sales down and high levels of debt. However, under the steer of former CEO, **Jørgen Vig Knudstorp**, the company transformed into a hugely profitable and popular global brand, thanks to radical interventions including: selling off its theme parks; reducing the number of pieces it produces by 50%; introducing new product ranges that appeal to a wider audience, including girls and adults; sustaining the brand through movies; and even crowdsourcing Lego ideas and designs via an innovation platform.[246]

Danish energy company **Ørsted** was able to evolve out of its old form, called Danish Oil and Natural Gas, after experiencing a financial crisis in 2012. Instead of going into 'recovery' mode by seeking to sustain and return to its previous state, the company sought to regenerate around a new core business focused on green energy rather than fossil fuels. In 2019, Ørsted was named by *Harvard Business Review* as one of the top 20 business transformations of the last decade.[247]

Reforested hillside, Calima, Valle del Cauca, Colombia. Deliberate intervention is needed in nature and organizations to ensure a healthy ecosystem. Once the right conditions for growth are created, natural processes respond.

Creating regenerative models of business

The idea of regenerative systems is starting to gain traction in different industries, as well as replacing sustainability as the main priority. While sustainability seeks to be efficient over the long term by maintaining the status quo, regeneration asks of us what the overall health of the system is, and what is actively being done to encourage a cycle of healing.[248]

As illustrated by systems thinker Anthony Hodgson, seeking to either sustain the current system or recover to a past state in the face of disruption will only result in degradation or collapse. More positively, a regenerative response that grows out of the old system will lead to a stronger form of resilience as the system itself evolves.[249]

Just as the forest holds within it the seeds for regrowth in the face of **Threats**, empowering it to respond to new opportunities, so can our own living systems nurture the capacity to regenerate. Many have started to explore and advocate for regenerative economies, agriculture and design, stating that what we create and how we do so needs to be considered across the full **Life cycle** and how this will impact people, nature, society, future generations, and so on.

John Fullerton, a former managing director at JP Morgan, has set up the **Capital Institute** and is a key leader in advocating for the regenerative economy as an evolution of our current mechanistic worldview. He characterizes a regenerative economy as one that:

- acts in ways that support the long-term health of society
- views economic and financial health as inseparable from human, societal and environmental health
- values richness of diversity, integrity and fairness
- seeks excellence through constructive competition
- responds to the full gamut of human needs, continually adapting to changing circumstances, and evolving to higher and more effective levels of organization.[250]

For organizations working specifically with manufacturing products, the application of regenerative thinking can provide new lines of business and revenue, as they close the loop for the 'end of life' phase of their products and reintegrate them back into their production system.

Far from being about 'just' recycling, regenerative thinking helps us to consider what resources we're taking in, how these change throughout their **Life cycle**, and what happens to them as they reach the end of that stage of the cycle. It encourages us to think about the **Relationship** of those products with the environment and their impact on people, and asks us to view ourselves and our actions as being part of nature, rather than outside it. Thought leader in regenerative planning, Bill Reed, depicts this in his blueprint for environmentally responsible design.[251]

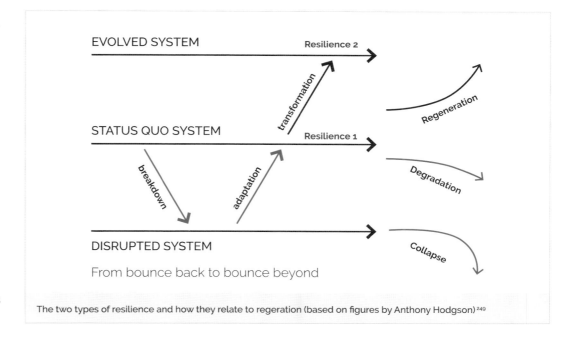

From bounce back to bounce beyond

The two types of resilience and how they relate to regeration (based on figures by Anthony Hodgson)[249]

Regeneration can spring up in the most surprising settings – including even the humble toilet. One of the more unlikely examples we've found is the redesign of the **public toilets at Kawakawa**, a small town in New Zealand. The town's toilets were redesigned by international architect **Friedensreich Hundertwasser**, who has a highly distinct and playful architectural style, reflected in the design; there is even a tree growing within the toilet block. This design initiative turned the formerly declining rural town into a thriving tourist stop-off, helping to regenerate the local economy and contributing to other urban renewal projects.[252]

Meanwhile, in Haiti, the **SOIL** (Sustainable Organic Integrated Livelihoods) initiative set up an inspiring scheme to support the sanitation crisis in that country. **EkoLakay**, a social business, provides affordable toilets and waste management services to 6,500 people, meeting ecological standards set by the World Health Organization and with 100 tons of compost from the scheme used to support agriculture and reforestation schemes.[253]

Kawakawa, North Island, New Zealand: the artistic and quirky Hundertwasser toilets are a tourist attraction.

Regenerating through renewed purpose

However, regeneration doesn't only need to be considered within the context of our impact on the environment.

We saw in **Purpose**, for example, how organizations are starting to rethink their core purpose to consider the role they play in wider society and to address the complex challenges facing both the Earth and human societies. And we saw in **Life cycles** how, with organizations on average surviving for fewer years than their predecessors, being able to adapt to changing environments is crucial.

A regenerative mindset – which is able to regrow in the face of destruction and anticipate next phases of evolution – is key to sensing those **Threats** and identifying the opportunities.

At a time when there is so much uncertainty and instability, knowing what the seeds of your next regeneration are in order to be able to adapt and transform at the right time is essential.

During the COVID-19 crisis there were many inspiring examples of individuals 'regenerating' their careers or organizations pivoting their activities. While this may have been driven by necessity, some have experienced a greater sense of purpose or discovered new business models that are likely to have life beyond the pandemic.

Within industries that have been heavily impacted, such as airlines and travel, some staff have taken up new roles within, for instance, supermarkets and food delivery, with some reporting having found a purpose and enjoyment they had not necessarily been expecting.[254]

Organizations that simply cannot operate in their normal way during lockdown have also turned to different business models and alternative revenue streams; for example, the iconic London live comedy venue **The Comedy Store** opened up its archives to relay shows online[255], while US hotel chain **Red Roof** offered low-cost day rates for its hotel rooms for remote workers to use as a quiet office during the day for people who were finding it hard to work from home.[256]

Others have revisited former projects. **Caspar Aremi** used to run a popular online LGBT magazine called **So So Gay**, which evolved from a personal blog. The magazine was discontinued in 2017 due to mounting costs but then, faced with a shortage of work during the pandemic, Aremi revisited So So Gay, this time creating a whole new online store specializing in underwear targeted to gay men and reintroducing elements of the magazine.[257]

Axolotl salamander, which can generate entire new limbs to replace those that have been damaged.

This renewed **Purpose** rings true no matter what level of the living system of work you're looking at. It could be the organization as a whole changing direction, or a region, division, specific team, or even an individual looking to learn new skills and adapt for the next stage of their career.

A regenerative mindset can see opportunities for new products and services that can grow out of the experience and expertise that already exist within the organization or could be integrated through new partnerships. And a forwarding-looking approach that looks out for what could be, rather than what was, means the organization can also play a role in regenerating its local community in the wake of a crisis.

Many of the Nature of Work elements have embedded deep within them the concept of regeneration: the need for **Biodiversity** across all its different facets, rethinking **Purpose**, adaptive **Structures**, flowing **Life cycles**, deep and broad **Relationships**, a deeper understanding of organizational **Health**, and the potential of **Threats** as opportunities.

Beneath all lies the idea that, as within nature, work as a living system is able to survive even as individual **Life cycles** come to an end, through new growth and evolution. The healthy forest renews and persists, in anticipation of natural threats and the death of its trees.

A regenerative organization is one that is constantly able to renew and evolve. Through this renewal, its long-term **Health** is maintained and ultimately improved. What's more, the regenerative organization seeks to make its surrounding environments healthier too, as its own longevity is reliant on the overall success of the systems on which it relies. This doesn't happen by chance; it happens by the people within that organization having a Nature of Work mindset and understanding the force that lies in regeneration. In doing this, they are able to look ahead to seek the organization's next evolution, as well as their own, particularly in moments of, or in anticipation of, crisis and disruption.

Ask yourself

- What regenerations have you been through in your own career? How did those regenerations come about? Do you know what the seeds of your next regeneration are?

- In the face of disruption and threats, do you and the people in your organization or work community tend to try to maintain and restore what's under threat, or do you seek opportunities for regeneration?

- Have parts of your organization – or your work community as a whole – been through any regenerations in the past? If so, what did that look like, what was involved and what was the impact?

- Are the seeds of regeneration already within your organization or work community? These could be through areas such as experimentation, innovation and feedback loops that help you to learn from and listen to your surrounding environments for potential threats.

- If there aren't seeds of regeneration, what can you do to help nurture them?

- Are there any opportunities in the products or services that your organization or work community creates to bring the final moments of those products or services' life cycle back in-house for reuse?

- What does your organization or work community do to play a role in supporting the regeneration of environments outside of itself, such as within society and natural habitats?

Intelligence

How will your organization harness intelligence, consciousness and (even) the sacred in work?

Nature: The ability in nature to receive information, and keep it as knowledge for future use, including by humans

Work: The integrated and collective consciousness (artificial, natural and human) of organizations and work communities

Humans have long looked to the stars in the hope of finding intelligent life, often forgetting that our planet teems with it.

The realm of artificial (and natural) intelligence

It has become something of artificial intelligence (AI) and robotics folklore to reference the use of friendly faced constructs in Japanese care homes to ease loneliness and provide company (albeit artificial) for the elderly population.[258] In fact, the last decade has seen a surge in intelligent systems across many different sectors, from ever smarter home management devices to the myriad applications now operating within manufacturing and distribution environments. Such use of machine learning and automation was already growing fast and the pandemic of 2020 has been a dramatic accelerant.

But the concept or vision of intelligence is far wider reaching within the realm of work than just automated help desks and intelligent searching, useful though such applications can be. When we step back, we can view any organization as a community of people seeking to achieve a shared result or experience. For example, take the Japanese care home. The collective **Purpose** is to provide the best service and experience for the residents; for them to be as happy and as well cared for as possible, with the community of staff, contractors, volunteers and visitors all seeking to achieve this in the most beneficial ways for everyone. Intelligence is required at all levels, and the more intelligent and conscious the system is, the richer the resulting experience and service will be. Just as with a human being, intelligence (not just innate but learned and cultivated) is a progressive attribute that flows into all aspects of life (and for organizations, into all aspects of work).

We are not alone

The search for what we might call higher or deeper intelligence can be observed at one end of the spectrum in the long-standing scientific space exploration quest to find tangible signs of microbes on our Solar System's planets[259], right

In his book *Are we smart enough to know how smart animals are?*, ethologist **Frans de Waal** makes the case for an expanded concept of intelligence, proposing that as humans we have become guilty of judging the natural world through our own experiences. Rather, different species (including our own) have evolved their own cognitive abilities, specifically adapted to their individual survival needs. De Waal's research shows us that to 'see' the unique intelligence of other organisms, we need first to cast aside our anthropomorphic worldview and develop instead empathy for all living beings.[220]

146

through to the more fanciful worlds of science fiction that have entertained and intrigued many generations. Both stem from humankind imagining that 'we are not alone', and that distant, intelligent, alien civilizations exist, probably with technology and a consciousness far advanced from our own.[260]

This seeming obsession with finding intelligent life beyond Earth hones in on a long history of humans trying to reconcile two seemingly opposing strands of thought. The first is a desire to understand ourselves in relation to some form of benevolent superior super- or non-human 'other', from whom we can learn. The story shared at the start of this book, from the film *Arrival*[7], bears witness to this deep desire for a benevolent, alien hand that can help us solve the many challenges our species, and indeed our planet, face. The second, conversely, is to understand ourselves as unique within the Cosmos, bequeathing humankind with an elevated status as the sole and supreme manifestation of intelligence.[261]

Our current hopes and fears around the technology we are creating – and in particular that infused with AI – in many ways mirror how people over centuries have processed this instinctive fascination with the concept of aliens: the hopes on the one hand that they will be able to save us, but on the other, the fears that, like Frankenstein's monster, our creations will turn on and destroy us.

And yet, as humankind looks to the future and how our relationship with intelligent technology will unfold, we all too often forget that already we are not alone. Rather, we are part of a planet teeming with intelligence. From the common spider in the corner of our room, whose web is an extension of its mind (*see pp.149-150*)[262], to the tusk fish in the ocean that uses tools[263], and so many more fascinating examples, planet Earth has evolved a whole array of alien-like intelligent life. It's just that many of us have forgotten how to see it.

Rediscovering ourselves as part of nature

For so long, and particularly within certain Western cultures, the ideas of 'intelligence' and 'consciousness' have been confined to what sets humans apart from the natural world. But the more we learn about those we share this planet with, the more we realize that these characteristics aren't 'sacred' to us exclusively but are found across Earth.

Each 'nature story' shared throughout this book bears within it a deep intelligence from which we can learn. The natural world – from the forest to the sea to the desert and beyond – thrums with emotion, cognition, consciousness and knowledge. Both creatures and plants have been found to have memory and to perceive the world around them for decision-making. A whole host of animals have been found to plan, grieve, experience joy, create tools, and so much more. Much of what we thought to be exclusively 'ours' is either shared, or manifests in forms almost beyond our comprehension.

For many, humankind has lost touch with this sense of a natural world that is truly alive, imbued with intelligence, sensitivity and empathy. However, as we move into the living

Mimosa pudica: a protective folding response means the leaves of the 'sensitive plant' will close when touched or shaken. However, if repeated touching doesn't result in any damage, after a while the plant stops reacting. The ability of plants to 'remember' past threats and adjust their behaviour accordingly shows they have a unique intelligence that we're only just beginning to understand.

age, we have an opportunity to rediscover a poetic and spiritual view of nature that can coexist with our emergent scientific knowledge of it. This combination of approaches will allow us better to understand how we, our intelligence capabilities, and that which we create, are all part of nature rather than separate from it.

Returning to the concept of myths touched upon at the start of this book, many Greek philosophers and storytellers perceived the natural world as 'alive' and intelligent, elevating the elements and Earth itself to the status of gods.[264] Shamanism, which can be understood as the spiritual traditions and practices of Indigenous Peoples, has been found to create experiences of greater connection with the consciousness of nature in all its forms.[265] Many more traditions and practices that bring humans back into the realm of the natural world exist across cultures and time.

Aligned with much of this thinking is an increased understanding of ourselves today as the ancestors of tomorrow, a mindset that for many cultures is central to their worldview. Both Bina Venkataraman (science policy expert and journalist)[266] and Roman Krznaric (philosopher)[267] have written about the need to think of ourselves as 'good ancestors', in order to bring us closer to the Earth we inhabit and that which future generations will inherit from us.

In rediscovering ourselves as being part of nature, we therefore create the opportunity to reconceptualize what intelligence is, and where it can be found.

Evolving a more integrated view of intelligence

What's more, our limited understanding of intelligence as a purely human – or superhuman – phenomenon not only harms our relationship with nature, but our **Relationships** with each other, and even with technology. In choosing to elevate some forms of intelligence above others, we miss opportunities to learn from each other and to create diverse work communities that can together find innovative solutions to a vast array of challenges, and so much more.

In creating a hierarchy of intelligence with 'mindless' nature at the bottom, ourselves in the middle, and the aspiration of intelligent machines at the top, we have placed ourselves at the centre of a tug-of-war of our own making.

Instead, we have the opportunity to discover a more rich, complex view of what intelligence is, flowing from an understanding of our own intelligence as part of nature, and the intelligence of machines as part of us.

The implications of this way of thinking for how we approach work is significant. This more fluid understanding of intelligence could help rebalance the fact that, for so long, certain types of work done by certain types of people have been elevated above others, instead of allowing us to recognize the full diversity of intelligence required across a whole host of work domains, from the home, to the street, to the shop floor, and beyond. This could help to create richer, more equitable and inclusive work communities.

This more integrated understanding of 'intelligence' could also assist us to root developments in AI, robotics and automation in more ethical thinking. Thus, it could help bring this nested system of intelligence together – machines, us, nature – as a collective consciousness that can span both time and physical space, in turn creating work communities that result in more purposeful and meaningful services, products and solutions.

Harnessing the wisdom of collective intelligence

This blending together of different intelligences isn't science fiction or far-fetched; it already exists in various forms around our globe. The connecting together of people over space and time, creating shared awareness and experiences, and accelerating social learning, has been enabled by the many tools we've created through the internet. Our own intelligence as individuals can, like never before, be combined with that of a huge diversity of other intelligences, liberating work from the confines of place and allowing it to become for many sectors and roles a globally shared experience.

The emergence of platforms that enable crowdfunding, crowdsourcing and petitions have all likewise helped to tap into this 'communal intelligence' that is created when groups of people are brought together with a shared **Purpose**.

Initiatives that may otherwise be unable to obtain funding through traditional means are suddenly possible through crowdfunding

platforms such as **Kickstarter**, **Indiegogo** and the many alternatives. Research that requires mass human analysis and problem-solving can be enabled through crowdsourcing platforms such as **Zooniverse**, which brings together volunteers to work on a whole range of research projects.[268] Work that would otherwise be impossible or hugely constrained by factors such as time, space and resources is suddenly possible in new ways.

As we saw in **Structures**, superorganisms can act as a single entity, despite consisting of individuals. There is an intelligence in the collective that can only emerge when those individuals come together through their **Relationships** and with shared **Purpose**. In this way, the organization can be viewed as having its own collective consciousness that is unique to it and is a result of how all its own Nature of Work elements combine to create an ecosystem.

Blended with both technology and an understanding of human intelligence as being part of nature, the size and capabilities of this collective can be immense. Leaders and change-makers who are able to behave as part of that collective will in coming years have a huge advantage over those who perceive themselves and act as superior and separate.

Rooting intelligence in ethics

While much good has come of harnessing the collective via technology, the technology itself is never neutral. Rather, it's created and used by people with their own biases, experiences and beliefs.

Spiders' webs have been found to work as an extension of their cognitive abilities, meaning their webs play a crucial role in how they perceive and understand the world around them.

Intelligence is also the lever that drives connections and networks, reflected in philosophies such as lifelong learning and movements like Working out Loud.

Isabel de Clercq, a thought leader on connected companies, comments: 'Organizations should know that they make part of an ecosystem. Connection with clients, employees and other stakeholders is critical to survival. I read a comment about how the CEO of Telefonica said there's no longer a digital and physical life, there's only one life. What has been flowing through our networks is not data, but stories, feelings and emotions.

Organizations and sometimes even departments still tend to think that they are self-sufficient entities. The predominant view is internally focused; this is why we have so many silos. But you also need a more outward-looking and external view.

When people can connect with others from different organizations that have the same problems, or are passionate about a topic, there is a desire to learn and share knowledge – and that is very powerful. A combination of a shared curiosity around a particular topic and a passion for lifelong learning is how connections are made.'[269]

The **Solarpunk** movement has emerged in recent years as a form of **utopic radical environmentalism**, infusing an optimistic view of the Earth's future with the potential benefits of technology, using art, fiction, fashion and other aesthetic media as forms of exploration.[270] Another strand approaches this 'techno-environmentalism' with the punk's attitude of rejecting today's status quo, rooted in activism in the here and now.[271]

This design prototype for Paris by architect Vincent Callebaut reimagines the future of the city with nature at its heart, integrating renewable and recyclable energies within its architecture and creating new eco-responsible ways of urban life.

In other words, the tools can only be as 'intelligent' – and ethical – as those creating them and using them.

That capability raises big questions for people in organizations: how do we enable and use this shared intelligence, while still protecting the rights and safety of individuals and of our wider environment? And how can we expand our own understanding of 'intelligence', so as to be inclusive and not project our own narrow beliefs about what does and doesn't comprise intelligence onto others?

As AI becomes more blended into our day-to-day lives, its potential to both neutralize and amplify human values, challenges and opportunities is immense. **Microsoft**'s 'AI for Good' initiative has identified five pillars through which AI can be harnessed for helping to solve humanitarian and environmental issues, covering:

- AI for Earth
- AI for Health
- AI for Accessibility
- AI for Humanitarian Action
- AI for Cultural Heritage.[272]

Within the workplace, AI is already being used to support areas such as the automation of certain tasks, analysis of huge data sets, recruitment and training.

And yet, there are already too many examples where the deployment of AI is reinforcing certain societal issues, rather than solving them. Facial recognition software,

Global pharmaceutical company **AstraZeneca** chose to develop its 2025 strategy, dubbed AZ2025, with input from employees. A three-week crowdsourcing initiative was held to involve as many of the company's 64,000 employees as possible, with ideas and contributions gathered via a plug-in which integrated with Workplace from Facebook. A high-profile campaign based around the tagline '**Think, Transform, Together**' was launched, involving management at both the global and local levels. The result was 77,000 interactions, 11,000 contributions and 23,000 ideas that have had a major influence on AstraZeneca's direction of travel.[273]

for example, has been found often to be coded by white engineers and 'trained' through machine learning with data sets that are frequently comprised of white faces. This has been found to disproportionality impact Black communities, particularly as facial recognition is increasingly being used within the justice system.[274]

Other fears are emerging around how 'intelligent' technology (whether this comprises a simple, non-AI powered algorithm or a fully enabled machine learning solution) is used, due to the potential impact on democracy[275], access to education[276], and even ethical dilemmas posed by self-driving cars when it comes to safety.[277] The impact of automation has also been found to be having an adverse impact on wages and job availability already in areas such as manufacturing.[278]

Methodologies such as human-centred design have long proposed the importance of creating products moulded to people's different needs, in collaboration with them. What is also increasingly required is a blended approach that recognizes the biases that are often unintentionally 'baked in' to solutions and experiences, together with a greater focus on potential unintended consequences of the technology that is in some areas evolving faster than society can keep up with.

AI specialists such as academic Josh Simons advocate for the application of three key considerations to AI solutions: fairness, accountability and privacy, as one way of tackling this challenge.[279] A study from McKinsey, which focused on the challenges around bias in

AI, likewise considered the impact of 'fairness', making six recommendations for maximizing fairness and minimizing bias. These are:

- Be aware of the contexts in which AI can help correct for bias as well as where there is a high risk that AI could exacerbate bias.
- Establish processes and practices to test for and mitigate bias in AI systems.
- Engage in fact-based conversations about potential biases in human decisions.
- Fully explore how humans and machines can best work together.
- Invest more in bias research, make more data available for research (while respecting privacy) and adopt a multidisciplinary approach.
- Invest more in diversifying the AI field itself.[280]

It can therefore be seen how the faith of many in the intelligence of technology – that elevation of it to the superhuman that can either save or destroy us – could be balanced out by rooting it in a more integrated view of intelligence that ultimately rediscovers us, as creators of technology, in nature.

The opportunities for augmenting human intelligence, as well as harnessing the collective consciousness of communities through technology, are huge, when the **Purpose** and impacts of that augmentation are properly thought through. For organizations experimenting with and creating digital workplaces that are increasingly going to be infused with AI, rooting the 'why' and the 'who' in the wider human, societal and natural impacts will be essential.

NeMO-Net is an innovative crowdsourcing initiative from **NASA** that is helping to train NASA's Pleiades supercomputer to better identify corals from underwater imaging technology. The ultimate aim is to accurately map the world's corals and understand the environmental impact so that coral can be better protected going forward.[281]

NASA has already developed an innovative video technology called **FluidCam** that involves underwater autonomous vehicles and produces high-resolution underwater imagery. So that the supercomputer can properly understand the images, an iPad-based game has been created where the public travel around in a fictional underwater research vessel and classify and colour 3D and 2D images. Modules train the players to improve their classification skills, unlock rewards and rate the efforts of other players. Machine learning extracts information from the public's classification in order to train the supercomputer to classify images on its own. The hope is that one day the technology may also assist in the search for life on other planets, including identifying areas of interest in the ancient dried-up seas of Mars.[282]

The beauty and mystery of a coral reef near the island of Aragusuku, Japan, which locals call the 'Palace of the Dragon King'. NASA has developed technology to help in the urgent need to identify and protect the world's threatened coral populations.

In recent years **NASA** has used **crowdsourcing** as a way to help generate ideas that can help its programmes, engage the public and even contribute to specific initiatives. This has been formalized within bodies across NASA, such as the Center of Excellence for Collaborative Innovation (CoECI), which helps to coordinate various 'challenges' to solve specific issues targeted at both specialists and the public. One vehicle for this is the **NASA Tournament Lab**, which uses a variety of open innovation platforms to come up with 'novel ideas or solutions to accelerate research and development efforts, improve algorithm performance, and seek new ideas and approaches in support of the NASA mission'.[283] Challenges that involve the public, where individuals have the opportunity to be 'citizen scientists' are listed at the **NASA SOLVE** website.[284] In addition, the **NASA@Work** programme organizes crowdsourcing initiatives involving NASA staff.[285]

What does your organization hold as sacred?

Recognizing your organization as a living system and approaching it with the Nature of Work mindset doesn't mean a rejection of technology.

Rather, for people looking to adapt their organizations for a living age, while still harnessing the many benefits of technology to support that 'collective consciousness', the blending together of the natural world, the human experience and the technological around an integrated and diverse concept of 'intelligence' could present a way forward.

What this often comes down to is the answer to the question: what do we hold as sacred in work? As we've seen throughout this book, for an increasing number of individuals and organizations, what is 'sacred' includes elements such as our shared and diverse human experiences, the environment, future generations and societal equity. The harnessing of collective intelligence in all its forms to those ends creates powerful opportunities for people to come together in new ways, enabled by the ability of humans to bridge the gap between nature and technology.

On the other hand, the elevation of elements such as technology, a narrow understanding of 'intelligence' and profit to the sacred, without living elements to temper them, is what has ultimately led to the harms of mechanistic work systems.

The Swedish word for business, *näringslivet*, if translated literally, means 'nourishment for life'.[9] If the living system of work is approached with this mindset – that it exists to nourish life – then it allows those in organizations to consider how the diverse intelligence of the collective can be harnessed to create that nourishment – for individuals, communities, interconnected living systems and even the natural world.

Ask yourself

- What's your own understanding and relationship with the concept of 'intelligence'? What does it include, and what does it exclude?

- How do you think and feel about artificial intelligence and emergent technologies? What are your hopes and fears about them?

- Are some forms of intelligence held to be more 'sacred' or elevated above others in your organization or work community? What are the different impacts of this?

- What could a more diverse and integrated understanding of intelligence mean for your organization or work community? Could it help create more equity? Could new forms of knowledge potentially be created?

- How does your organization or work community consider ethics in relation to intelligence? Could you and your colleagues develop a renewed commitment to ethics?

- How could the integrated 'humans as part of nature; machines as part of humans' view of intelligence influence the way that people in your organization or work community approach work, people, nature and technology?

- How could your organization or work community harness collective intelligence across communities for inclusive and innovative problem-solving?

Health

What do the health indicators in your organization reveal?

Nature: A measure of inter-related factors to determine the condition of a natural element

Work: The many living factors that contribute to the longevity of an organization

A new understanding of organizational health

Global investor **Blackrock** has one of the largest and most financially successful portfolios of investments in the world. In January 2020, its CEO Larry Fink announced to the financial community that going forward it will only make investments in companies that meet its criteria for environmental, social and political risk, and that it was integrating sustainability into its core requirements.[286]

This was certainly newsworthy but not too surprising. What would have seemed completely implausible in 2010 now felt just like a forward-looking shift in policy, with Fink referencing the climate change movement and protests of 2019 as he pointed to a 'fundamental reshaping of finance'. When a firm that manages around $7 trillion (yes, trillion) in assets suggests a fundamental reshaping economically, many traditional organizations pay keen attention.

What might such a transformation in finance look like?

Around the same time, **Microsoft** committed itself not only to becoming carbon negative by 2030 but to have removed by 2050 all the carbon it has ever produced since it was founded in 1975.[287]

Now, we can debate the motivations and realities of both these commitments. Nevertheless, they are reflective of a new way of considering organizations and their health. In each case, the 'health' of the company is being extended into areas far beyond the common notion of 'financial health'. If all that matters is the single economic health indicator, why seek to repair the climate damage caused in the past 50 years or so by Microsoft, as this will be expensive, difficult and most likely open to criticism? Both actions speak of a broader comprehension of 'health' in the respective organizations.

The concept of the **triple bottom line (TBL)** was created in 1994 by **John Elkington**, as a framework that sought to apply accounting principles not just to economic health and performance, but also to the environmental and social impacts of an organization.

While the concept took off, Elkington himself in 2018 suggested the framework needed a 'recall', saying that it had been diluted by those still following a single bottom line mindset.[288]

The 'living' health of forests

As we embark on our final Nature of Work element, **Health**, we pause to consider the journey we have travelled together through so many aspects of nature to reach this point. And so, before we follow this final trail, let's take a moment to experience where we find ourselves.

Imagine yourself within a vibrant, rich, flourishing forest. You're standing, or sitting, or lying down on the forest floor. It's springtime and, as you close your eyes, you can sense the living system of the forest unfurling around you. The creaking, ancient sound of trees, their branches and leaves moving with the wind. The sound of songbirds calling out to one another. The gentle breeze on your skin. The complex scents of the forest, of the bark, the pollen, a slight dampness, the crispness of the air. As you open your eyes, the colours of the forest in spring burst forth: the greens, pinks, blues, gentle browns.

The health of the forest is all around you: a living, dynamic, interconnected superorganism, ebbing and flowing between the points of regeneration and death.

So many different elements must combine to make this ecosystem healthy: the **Biodiversity** of the many plants and creatures that call it home, their **Relationships** of mutualism, and adaptive and responsive **Structures**; the **Roots** that stretch out beneath your feet underground, through which nourishment and communication flow; the **Life cycles** gradually unfolding over days, months, years, decades,

and even millennia; the **Regeneration** that flows out of these life cycles; and the **Threats**, which help all to keep in balance. Then there are the **Migrations** of the creatures that come and go, drawn at various times to this or that **Habitat**. Meanwhile, all of this is underpinned by the deep, interconnected **Purpose** and myriad different forms of **Intelligence** that combine to help the forest and its many inhabitants survive.

The health of the forest is not located in one thing. Rather, it's the cumulative effect of all these elements. Any one of these, if under **Threat**, can put the whole ecosystem at risk. It's a system that sounds precarious, delicate. And yet, it's one that has been resilient over timescales almost unfathomable to us.

And now, picture another forest, also in spring. The birds have fallen silent. There is no rich orchestra of leaves rustling, for they too have gone. There is just the sound of the wind – and a smell of decay, carried on that wind. Around you, trees with dead roots either stand bare and forlorn or have been felled. There are no shoots of new life. All is a desolate dark brown, grey. The forest has died.

What separates these two images is health; from good health to ill health, and ultimately death. The latter is a scene that many fear is unfolding across our planet, whether from the climate crisis, aggressive human development resulting in deforestation, or forestry practices that are neither sustainable nor regenerative.

The health of living systems is complex, just like the health of organisms. Both amount to the

Dead forest, Manasquan Reservoir, New Jersey, US. Organizations also have a life cycle that can come to an end if this cycle is disrupted by threats resulting in health deteriorating to the point of extinction. The impact on communities can be devastating.

cumulative effect of many different factors. A deep understanding of these health influences is what paints the full picture of the existential threats to our planetary and organizational health. Investigating this area is also where we can find new resources and resilience.

For the human species, as inhabitants of this Earth who both impact and are impacted by the health of nature's ecosystems, it takes more than one kind of knowledge and **Intelligence** to recognize the complexities of its health and to understand how we can act to help nurture **Regeneration**.

Rather, it takes the collective and combined knowledge, wisdom, experience and imagination of multiple cultures, specialisms and intelligences to bring that full story of health together, not only for our forests and the multitude of other natural ecosystems, but also for the world of work.

The lesson for us and the Nature of Work is that the health of living systems is not one-dimensional; no one person or measure is able fully to assess how healthy an organization is. Instead, it takes those in the work community to come together as witnesses to the state of an organization's health, with a range of experts collaborating to interpret what the indicators mean, in turn enabling connected change agents to transform that knowledge into action.

A holistic view of organizational health

It has always been natural for us to be concerned with our own individual health.

We experience ourselves as living entities, and our understanding of what good health entails continues to evolve rapidly as we gain a deeper sense of what makes for a healthy human.

Interestingly, there is a long history of taking mental and emotional states into consideration as a part of 'health', going back as far as the Ancient Greeks and Romans.[289] And yet, Western medicine and healthcare have largely evolved to focus narrowly on the biological processes underlying illness and disease, being overwhelmingly concerned with the individual physical body and often ignoring many other potential health factors. Practices from other cultures on the other hand, such as those in Asia, have historically sought to understand health in a wider way, relating it to elements such as social **Relationships**, societal norms and ecological factors.[290] These different traditions – from individualist to collectivistic – bring both opportunities and challenges for how we consider the health of a living system, from the smallest part of it up to the full system.

And yet, this rich, accumulative knowledge of health, evolved over thousands of years and across different traditions, is seemingly abandoned when we consider both people in the workplace and the health of the organization itself.

Whichever approach to human health is adopted, when humans enter the workplace to collaborate with other people and work using technologies and systems, they have historically been reduced to 'parts' of a machine, with the collective effect of each of these parts adding

When the Fukuoka Prefectural International Hall, Kyushu, Japan, was built, the equivalent natural environment that would be lost to accommodate the building was incorporated in a vertical garden of the same total area. In a living age, such imaginative approaches to blending human-made worlds and structures with nature are needed to protect the health of both.[291]

up to a complex mechanical unit. And what's more, the health indicators of that unit have been limited to the simplest outcome. Does the machine function? If so, that means it 'works'. This is as much 'organizational health' as we have typically been concerned with.

But once we start to regard this gathering of many humans, plus the processes and tools with which they work, as living systems with their own dynamic ecology, then health is liberated from the constraints of the machine to evolving as an exhilarating new conception of what a healthy organization – or a healthy organism – looks like.

We have grown used to the term 'financial health' and we have refined balance sheets where we can see at a glance whether an organization is financially in robust health or at a point of risk. But what if we had a full range of health indicators across the many other elements that make up its health, such as the Nature of Work elements, and many more?

Finding new indicators of your organization's health

As we saw in **Structures**, a tight focus on productivity and output was a key feature of the industrial age, when people were physically

Since 2000, **Edelman** has studied how 'trust' in four major societal institutions has fluctuated globally, and why. Looking at government, business, media and non-governmental organizations (NGOs), the study concludes that there are two essential elements to trust: effectiveness (*delivering on promises*) and ethical behaviour (*doing the right thing and working to improve society*). Based on findings from its 2020 Trust Barometer (conducted prior to COVID-19), key trends have emerged:

- A growing sense of inequity is undermining trust.

- There is a sense of deep-seated fear about the future; 83% of employees fear losing their jobs due to a number of causes.
- The public doesn't trust NGOs, businesses and governments to effectively partner together to solve the complex societal challenges we face.

While businesses were seen as being more competent, NGOs were viewed as more ethical. And yet, ethical drivers were found to be three times more important in contributing to trust in a company than competence.[292]

UK travel operator **Virgin Trains** ditched the annual employee engagement survey altogether and took some time to figure out a better way of tracking employee wellbeing and sentiment. The company hired a third party to carry out in-depth interviews with employees in their homes and identified four main trends that matter – trust, empowerment, passion and stress. They then introduced an app called **Vibe**, which tracks how employees feel across these four aspects, using a combination of more traditional questions with psychometric testing, involving reactions to different images.[293]

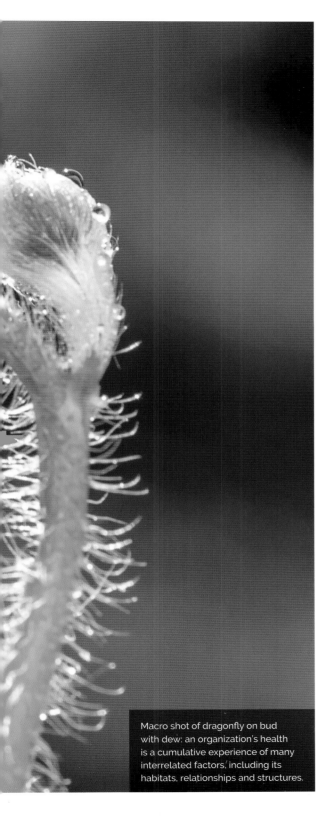

Macro shot of dragonfly on bud with dew: an organization's health is a cumulative experience of many interrelated factors,' including its habitats, relationships and structures.

making 'products' that could be easily counted both in terms of quantity and the time taken to manufacture them.

This is a legacy that has stayed with us, even as the types of work people engage in have expanded from those with more easily measurable outputs. In its research looking into *People, Productivity and the Digital Workplace* (2018), **BT** found that 81% of executives responding to a survey claimed that: 'Improving employee productivity is our top priority', with 91% believing that: 'Productivity is the main benefit of improving digital experiences.[294]

That word 'productivity' is one that is increasingly difficult to define as one thing though, particularly for people who aren't directly working in manufacturing or operating in billable hours. It's an assessment of how effective someone is in completing a task, often with economic efficiency a prioritized indicator of health.

And yet, despite this, as we moved deeper into the 20th and 21st centuries, there *have* been attempts to define different approaches to organizational health, based on the understanding that it reflects a myriad of factors that can be taken as key indicators.

Organizational Development theory, for example, born in the 1930s and finessed in the 1950s, was underpinned by humanistic values such as whether an organization was providing opportunities for people to function as human beings, each with a complex set of needs.[295]

Diagnostics have also emerged from organizations such as McKinsey, which has developed an 'Organizational Health Index' that identifies nine dimensions of 'health', with an associated 39 management practices. As the McKinsey team writes: 'Organizational health is organic, and, like the human body, it evolves over time. If health is to be nurtured and improved quickly, it needs to be monitored and measured regularly.'[296]

Quarterly fiscal reporting therefore won't help provide such insights into the organization's health. McKinsey recommends instead seeking tools and methods to check in with people daily, through weekly health huddles, and by running specific health-focused reviews across the indicators that have been selected for your organization.

And yet, time and again, that same measure of fiscal health will be the one that is elevated above others. Fiscal health is, of course, crucial; it pays people's salaries, and means resources, tools, and so on, can be purchased. But additional factors – such as the Nature of Work elements covered in this book – can also be elevated to recognize the key role they play in organizational health, accompanied by new thinking around qualitative and quantitative ways of creating and tracking relevant indicators.

Community health and wellbeing

Approaches developed to assess and manage the health and wellbeing of communities can also be turned to as sources of potential

For nations and governments, wellbeing is increasingly emerging as a measure of overall health for the nation alongside the more traditional GDP. **New Zealand**, for example, released its first **Wellbeing Budget** in 2019, stating: 'Our five Wellbeing Budget priorities show how we have broadened our definition of success for our country to one that incorporates not just the health of our finances, but also of our natural resources, people and communities', with wellbeing defined as: 'When people are able to lead fulfilling lives with purpose, balance and meaning to them.'[297]

After a consultation period, multiple indicators of wellbeing across the domains of its **Living Standards Framework** were identified. A dashboard that reports on progress against each of the wellbeing measures is available for public viewing online, and represents a new way of discussing and quantifying the health of the country across non-financial wellbeing indicators.[298]

inspiration for developing new ways of thinking about organizational health, based on understanding the organization as a community of people and **Relationships**.

While interest has increased in individual wellbeing along with wellbeing at the national level as measures of 'health', a gap was identified in 'community wellbeing' as a way of understanding the areas that impact 'being well together'. In other words, there are communal factors related to how people within the **Structures** of a community interact with and impact each other, together with environmental factors, that should be taken into consideration.

A study into community wellbeing conducted in the UK over 5 years found a whole host of indicators, frameworks and measures in use by both government agencies and NGOs, covering a range of community wellbeing indicators across domains such as health and wellbeing, economy, inclusion and **Relationships**.[299]

The study also found four areas crucial to community wellbeing that are often left out of frameworks: environmental sustainability, inequality, considerations of cultural heritage and intergenerational relations.[299]

Each of these could potentially be mapped to a Nature of Work element: **Regeneration**; **Biodiversity**; **Roots**; and both **Life cycles** and **Relationships**. This helps show how a mindset that considers organizations as living systems could help people within those organizations to deepen their understanding of what a healthy living system looks and 'feels' like, to support strategy and decision-making around managing

that organization's health. Likewise, it can help build a picture of what one suffering ill health looks like, and what the contributing factors to that might be.

Individual health and wellbeing

Emergent practices, such as mental health awareness and first aid[300], together with programmes focused on individual wellbeing, have become increasingly common within organizations in recent years. Facilities such as these are aimed at addressing the mental health impact of work as well as creating more inclusive environments, where people will feel safe sharing their mental health and wellbeing challenges.

Other practices, such as more frequent touchpoints with managers to enable them to build trusting relationships with their teams, have also emerged as a way of quickly identifying where someone's wellbeing is potentially being impacted by work, or by factors outside of work, and how to support that person rather than punish them for any impact these events might be having on their performance.

With the onset of the COVID-19 pandemic, organizational responsibility for people's physical and mental health came even more to the forefront, both in terms of how physically safe environments were for the people expected to work in them, but also the extent to which leaders, managers and colleagues were able to empathize with the physical and mental wellbeing of others in their organization and

Initiatives such as the **Mental Health at Work Commitment** encourage organizations to adopt a framework designed to help remove the stigma of talking about mental health at work, and promote cultures, tools and practices that drive good mental health. These core commitments ask organizations to:

- Prioritize mental health in the workplace by developing and delivering a systematic programme of activity.
- Proactively ensure that work design and organizational culture drive positive mental health outcomes.
- Promote an open culture around mental health.
- Increase organizational confidence and capability.
- Provide mental health tools and support.
- Increase transparency and accountability through internal and external reporting.[301]

In a process called 'phototropism' certain flowers turn to face the sun throughout the day to enhance their health by capturing energy through photosynthesis.[302]

The overall health of a system is reliant on each of its elements functioning well and being in balance. *Illustration by Liad Janes*

wider community. It threw into stark relief the need for working environments and relationships that view and support people in their entirety.

The health of the ecosystem of work

This 'living system' approach to organizational health not only helps to take into account the wellbeing of the individual, and of individuals together, but can also help people to understand how societal factors such as inequity manifest within their organization, and indeed how they themselves might contribute to this. Combined with practices and indicators associated with elements such as **Purpose**

and **Threats**, a much broader definition of organizational health can be uncovered.

Developing an organization's own Nature of Work health indicators across the dimensions of the individual, its different communities, the organization as a whole, and then within the context of its role in society, can help build up a richer picture of how healthy the organizational ecosystem actually is.

Without having the right health indicators to monitor, understand and act upon, it can often be too late when it is picked up that an organization has reached a state of ill-health. As we saw in **Life cycles**, understanding what the decline of an organization looks like, and the

impact of this, can help to sharpen attentiveness towards its state of health. We can then aim to introduce 'preventative' measures and seek the right interventions before the symptoms become too serious.

This living understanding of organizational health will help people to create work communities that add to their own health as well as that of their colleagues and society, rather than acting in ways that work against it. And, ultimately, this is what the **Nature of Work** is about: healthy, vibrant organizations that flourish as living systems through which their people and society can in turn thrive together.

Ask yourself

- When you look at your organization or work community, does it seem 'healthy' to you? Which parts seem to be in good health, and which parts seem to be suffering ill health?

- Which health indicators do you and people in your organization or work community seem to currently prioritize, based on the reports used for decision-making and the areas where budget is allocated? Why are these areas considered important?

- Are there Nature of Work elements that you and those around you haven't considered to be important to the health

of the organization or work community before? If so, why is that?

- What could a new list of health indicators, which align with the Nature of Work mindset, look like for your organization or work community? What are the different (ethical) qualitative and quantitative ways that they can be tracked to support decision-making?

- What would these new health indicators mean for your people, and their own health and wellbeing? And what could they mean for the organization's impact on wider society?

Reflections

One of the trips I, Paul, love is an annual visit to Cornwall in the southwest of England. The journey from our home in the Cotswolds countryside (which, while beautiful, is a long way from any sea) has a thrilling quality through the anticipation of the ocean that will eventually come into view. We take a bend in the road and there it is, the Atlantic Ocean, stretching out in front of us, the sight we've longed for.

For both myself and Shimrit, the journey of researching and writing this book has been regenerative; who we were when we started out, with just the seed of an idea in our first conversations in 2019, isn't who we are now as we finish writing. The story told within these pages has transformed both our own relationships with work, and with nature itself. Within both, we feel a deep sense of awe and hope as to what could be possible. Sometimes, the story doesn't only change the listeners but the storytellers too.

In many conversations, our headline description of this book has generated reactions of encouragement, even excitement. Particularly for the aspiring leaders of the future, the premise of **Nature of Work** has captured their attention. The idea that where we work is alive, more like a natural living system or forest, seems to touch us personally as well as professionally in 2020. The book's perspective acts like a vision towards the horizon of a scene not yet witnessed, but one those we've talked to know with surety exists. An expanse of ocean just around the corner, in touching distance.

A more beautiful world of work

On reflection, this book describes a way of working and organizing that carries the seeds of a potentially 'more beautiful world of work our hearts know is possible'[303] and one that is essential for our collective futures. 'More of the same' is a road we know leads to a dead end. Listening to many comments, it is clear that Nature of Work constitutes a yearning for a far more rewarding, purposeful, dignified, connected and regenerative way of working.

Beginning this adventure in the middle of 2019 (a year when climate activism came of age and 16-year-old environmental activist Greta Thunberg was voted by *Time* magazine their 'Person of the Year', the youngest ever winner) felt timely. But then what 2020 brought in the form of our first global pandemic since the Spanish Flu a century before has been an accelerant. The notion that organizations are alive came into stark relief and the relevance of this new story of work for a living age felt increasingly relevant.

The next question...

What is intriguing and urgent now is to see how organizations of all sizes, and perhaps particularly the largest ones, start to adapt and evolve as the Nature of Work narrative gains influence. With Nature of Work as a call to action, what practical changes will people in organizations enact that reflect a natural way of working? How will their approach to stakeholders expand? What will their supply chain look like? What approaches will they take with the human beings they employ or contract with? How will they define growth in fresh, new and dynamic ways? And how will they evolve their role and purpose in society?

Our hope is that this book will help initiate a movement towards a collectively beneficial way of working; that change-makers treat the book as a shared story with which they can engage in their own organizations and work communities, and in collaboration with others. Shifting the direction of travel for an economic and industrial system that stretches back centuries is not a quick adjustment – but we live in urgent times where we know we must enable deep-lying transformations in so many aspects of how we live. Hopefully, Nature of Work can help us on this connected journey.

Ask yourself

- How do you feel, having finished this book?
- How has Nature of Work impacted you and how you think and feel about work?
- Have any of the elements or 'stories' resonated with you more deeply than others? What was it you particularly connected with?
- How will you take on these Nature of Work stories and live them in your own life, and within your own organization or work community? What will you be doing differently now to what you did before?
- Who will you share Nature of Work with, and how, and why?
- Which Nature of Work stories were missing and how can you help them to be told?

Afterword

Charles Eisenstein

Author of: *Climate – A New Story, Sacred Economics* and *The More Beautiful World Our Hearts Know is Possible*.

This book has been about aligning work with Nature. However, most of what it says about economic work applies equally to work conceived more broadly as our participation in the world. The question 'What is your real work here?' reaches far beyond professional life.

Collectively, the answer to that question is changing. Civilization has long understood its work to be the expansion of the human realm – domesticating the wild and ordering chaotic reality with technology. Now, surveying the resulting desolation, we turn toward a new purpose: to heal the damage and serve the next unfolding of life and beauty on Earth.

This purpose entails a bottom-up reconception of what work is. Work has a scientific as well as an economic definition. In physics, work is the product of force and mass; for example, work is done when a mass is accelerated over a distance.

In the 'old story' of man versus Nature, humanity's progress meant advancing in our capacity to do this kind of work. Animal power, and then the machine, enabled us to move a lot more mass a lot further. Humanity's ability to impose its design onto Nature grew exponentially, yet somehow, the promised paradise never materialized.

Today, it is evident that our planetary crisis cannot be resolved by harnessing more energy to further dominate the material world.

When we understand that Nature too has purpose and intelligence, another possibility for human progress – and therefore for work – presents itself. Rather than conquering Nature and dominating the material world, we can work in alignment with Nature's purpose. What makes that work powerful is no longer the amount of force we can bring to bear; it is the sensitivity of our perception. Tuning into an intelligence and purpose beyond ourselves, whether of an organization or the whole of life on Earth, we become able to accomplish very much with very little.

Paul and Shimrit observe early in this book that more people than ever – 35% – feel engaged by their work. That still leaves 65% who do not. Industrial work involved not only the subordination of Nature to man, but also the subordination of human to machine. Thus, we became cogs in that machine. The future of work is to become more like cells in an organism or species in an ecosystem, each exercising their gifts to the highest capacity so that life can flourish.

Sources

All urls correct at time of going to print, November 2020.

How to use this book

1. Shimrit Janes. *Nature of Work: Designing at the interface of the physical and digital workplace*. DWG Research, 2019 (digitalworkplacegroup.com/resources/download-reports/nature-of-work-designing-at-the-interface-of-the-physical-and-digital-workplace).

2. Shutterstock. *The ultimate guide to the Golden Ratio and how to apply it to your designs*. Shutterstock Blog, Sep 8, 2017 (www.shutterstock.com/blog/what-is-the-golden-ratio).

3. Paul Miller. *The digital workplace: How technology is liberating work*. TECL Publishing, 2012 (digitalworkplacebook.com).

4. Cision PR Newswire. *Digital workplace market worth $35.7 billion by 2023*. Exclusive report by MarketsandMarkets™ (www.prnewswire.co.uk/news-releases/digital-workplace-market-worth-35-7-billion-by-2023-exclusive-report-by-marketsandmarkets-tm--800867913.html).

Why Nature of Work?

5. CNN. *People in India can see the Himalayas for the first time in 'decades,' as the lockdown eases air pollution*. CNN Travel, Apr 9, 2020 (edition.cnn.com/travel/article/himalayas-visible-lockdown-india-scli-intl/index.html).

6. Caitlyn Collins, et al. *COVID-19 and the gender gap in work hours*. Gender, Work & Organization, Jul 2, 2020: 1–12 (doi.org/10.1111/gwao.12506).

7. Wikipedia. *Arrival (film)* (en.wikipedia.org/wiki/Arrival_(film)).

8. Rita Gunther McGrath. *Management's three eras: A brief history*. Harvard Business Review, Jul 30, 2014 (hbr.org/2014/07/managements-three-eras-a-brief-history).

9. Arie de Geus. *The living company: Habits for survival in a turbulent business environment*. Harvard Business School Press, 1997 (www.ariedegeus.com).

10. Giles Hutchins. *The nature of business: Redesigning for resilience*. Green Books, 2012 (thenatureofbusiness.org/2014/04/23/the-nature-of-business-redesigning-for-resilience-in-an-increasingly-volatile-world).

11. Rodger Dean Duncan. *The why of work: Purpose and meaning really do matter*. Forbes: Leadership, Sep 11, 2018 (www.forbes.com/sites/rodgerdeanduncan/2018/09/11/the-why-of-work-purpose-and-meaning-really-do-matter).

12. PwC. *People power your business*. PwC: Workplace of the Future (www.pwc.com/us/en/library/workforce-of-the-future/fulfillment-at-work.html).

13. Edelman. *2020 Edelman Trust Barometer Spring update: Trust and the COVID-19 pandemic*. Daniel J Edelman Holdings, Inc., 2020 (www.edelman.com/research/trust-2020-spring-update).

14. Fernando Duarte. *Black Lives Matter: Do companies really support the cause?* BBC World Service, Jun 13, 2020 (www.bbc.com/worklife/article/20200612-black-lives-matter-do-companies-really-support-the-cause).

15. DWG. *Walmart – inside (probably) the world's biggest intranet*. Digital Workplace Impact podcast, Ep 49, 2020 (digitalworkplacegroup.com/dwg_podcast/walmart-intranet).

16. Paul Miller. *Decade of Courage manifesto*. DWG Research, 2020 (digitalworkplacegroup.com/resources/download-reports/decade-of-courage-manifesto).

17. The World Bank. *Labor force, total*. The World Bank data, derived from International Labour Organization, ILOSTAT database on Jun 21, 2020 (data.worldbank.org/indicator/SL.TLF.TOTL.IN).

What is Nature of Work?

18. Leyla Acaroglu. *Tools of a system thinker*. Medium.com, Sep 7, 2017 (medium.com/disruptive-design/tools-for-systems-thinkers-the-6-fundamental-concepts-of-systems-thinking-379cdac3dc6a).

19. Sam Woolfe. *The human need for storytelling*. SamWoolfe.com, Sep 30, 2019 (www.samwoolfe.com/2019/09/the-human-need-for-storytelling.html).

20. Fritjof Capra, Pier Luigi Luisi. *The systems view of life: A unifying vision*. Cambridge University Press, 2014 (www.cambridge.org/core/books/systems-view-of-life/35186BA5B12161E469C4224B6076ADFE).

21. Vasyl Shynkaruk, et al. *Myth as a phenomenon of culture*. National Academy of Managerial Staff of Culture and Arts Herald, Nov 2018 (www.researchgate.net/publication/329992241_MYTH_AS_A_PHENOMENON_OF_CULTURE).

22. Manuel Lima. *The book of trees: Visualizing branches of knowledge*. New York: Princeton Architectural Press, 2014.

23. Jeremy Coles. *How nature is good for our health and happiness*. BBC Earth, Apr 20, 2016 (www.bbc.co.uk/earth/story/20160420-how-nature-is-good-for-our-health-and-happiness).

24. Edward O Wilson. *Biophilia*. Cambridge: Harvard University Press. 1984.

25. Biomimicry Institute. *For all the challenges we face, nature has a solution*, 2020 (biomimicry.org/what-is-biomimicry).

26. Sue Thomas. *Technobiophilia: Nature and cyberspace*. Bloomsbury Academic. 2013 (suethomasnet.wordpress.com/technobiophilia).

27. Gareth Morgan. *Images of organization*. Thousand Oaks, CA, Sage Publications, Inc., 2006.

28. Ken Thompson. *Bioteams*. Meghan Kiffer Press, 2008.

Purpose

29. Strawberry Frog & Reputation Institute. *Welcome to the Purpose Power Index™* (www.purposepowerindex.com).

30. Editors of Encyclopaedia Britannica. *Fruit*. Britannica (www.britannica.com/science/fruit-plant-reproductive-body).

31. Iza Kavedžija. *The Japanese concept of ikigai: Why purpose might be a better goal than happiness*. The Conversation, Dec 14, 2017 (theconversation.com/the-japanese-concept-of-ikigai-why-purpose-might-be-a-better-goal-than-happiness-88709).

32. Munyaradzi Mawere. *On pursuit of the purpose of life: The Shona metaphysical perspective*. Mozambique, Universidade Pedagogica, Journal of Pan African Studies, 2010, 3(6): 269–84 (www.researchgate.net/publication/228672254_On_Pursuit_of_the_Purpose_Life_The_Shona_Metaphysical_Perspective).

33. Ilene Berns-Zare. *The importance of having a sense of purpose*. Psychology Today, Jun 4, 2019 (www.psychologytoday.com/gb/blog/flourish-and-thrive/201906/the-importance-having-sense-purpose).

34. Interview with Florin Rotar, Modern Workplace Global Lead, Avanade, July 2020.

35. Jim Harter. *4 factors driving record-high employee engagement in US*. Gallup, Feb 4, 2020 (www.gallup.com/workplace/284180/factors-driving-record-high-employee-engagement.aspx).

36. Samantha Todd. *The 'why' behind our work: What is 'purpose,' and do we need it?* Forbes: Leadership Strategy, Jul 29, 2019 (www.forbes.com/sites/samanthatodd/2019/07/29/the-why-behind-our-work-what-is-purpose-and-do-we-need-it/#e91a6d912651).

37. Riverford. *Employee ownership*. Riverford Organic Farmers: Ethics and ethos (www.riverford.co.uk/ethics-and-ethos/employee-ownership).

38. Karianne Gomez, et al. *Understanding Generation Z in the workplace*. Deloitte: Perspectives (www2.deloitte.com/us/en/pages/consumer-business/articles/understanding-generation-z-in-the-workplace.html).

39. Sally Ho. *Generation Alpha: 67% of 6–9 year olds want to make saving the planet their career mission*. Green Queen, Oct 16, 2019 (www.greenqueen.com.hk/generation-alpha-67-of-6-9-year-olds-want-to-make-saving-the-planet-their-career-mission).

40. Elspeth Taylor. *Pandemic influences kids' career aspirations*. Stylus: The Brief, Apr 30, 2020 (www.stylus.com/pandemic-influences-kids-career).

41. Michael T Warren. *How teens are making meaning out of the pandemic*. Greater Good Magazine: Education, Sep 16, 2020 (greatergood.berkeley.edu/article/item/how_teens_are_making_meaning_out_of_the_pandemic).

42. Who Gives a Crap. *About us* (uk.whogivesacrap.org/pages/about-us).

43. Xylem. *About Watermark* (www.xylem.com/en-uk/watermark).

44. Shimrit Janes. *What digital workplace practitioners can learn from the Tech for Good movement*. DWG website: News, Aug 28, 2019 (digitalworkplacegroup.com/2019/08/28/what-digital-workplace-practitioners-can-learn-from-the-tech-for-good-movement).

45. Diana O'Brien, et al. *Purpose is everything: How brands that authentically lead with purpose are changing the nature of business today*. Deloitte: Insights, Oct 15, 2019 (www2.deloitte.com/us/en/insights/topics/marketing-and-sales-operations/global-marketing-trends/2020/purpose-driven-companies.html).

46. Cassie Robinson. *Beyond human-centred design, to?* Medium.com, Dec 26, 2018 (medium.com/@cassierobinson/beyond-human-centred-design-to-501a994f3123).

47. Unilever. *The Unilever Sustainable Living Plan* (www.unilever.co.uk/sustainable-living/the-unilever-sustainable-living-plan).

48. Unilever. *Brands with purpose grow – and here's the proof*. Unilever: News & Features, Jun 11, 2019 (www.unilever.co.uk/news/news-and-features/2019/brands-with-purpose-grow-and-here-is-the-proof.html).

49. David Molloy. *Coronavirus: Tech firm Bloom Energy fixes broken US ventilators*. BBC News: Technology, Mar 30, 2020 (www.bbc.co.uk/news/technology-52094193).

50. Estee Lauder Companies. *The Estée Lauder Companies contribute to global COVID-19 relief support*. Company Feature, Jul 8, 2020 (www.elcompanies.com/en/news-and-media/newsroom/company-features/2020/COVID-19-efforts).

51. Medea Giordano. *The nonprofits and companies helping to fight the pandemic*. Wired, May 7, 2020 (www.wired.com/story/covid-19-charities-nonprofits-companies-helping).

Roots

52. Daniel Ranta, GE. *Knowledge sharing at GE*. Digital Workplace Experience: Live Tour, Jun 21, 2019 (www.slideshare.net/dwexperience/live-tour-knowledge-sharing-at-ge-daniel-ranta).

53. Greg McCoy. *Procter & Gamble Heritage Center and Archives*. Society of American Archivists (www2.archivists.org/groups/business-archives-section/repository-profile-procter-gamble).

54. DFS. *Our Business*. DFS: Careers (www.dfscareers.co.uk/our-business.html).

55. Tessy Koshy. *Inside my job: The corporate historian*. Friday, Nov 29, 2017 (fridaymagazine.ae/life-culture/people-profiles/inside-my-job-the-corporate-historian-1.2131737).

56. Robert Hudson Westover. *Methuselah, a bristlecone pine is thought to be the oldest living organism on Earth*. US Department of Agriculture, Feb 21, 2017 (www.usda.gov/media/blog/2011/04/21/methuselah-bristlecone-pine-thought-be-oldest-living-organism-earth).

57. Discover the Daintree. *About the Daintree Rainforest* (www.discoverthedaintree.com/daintree-rainforest-6).

58. USDA. *Pando – I spread*. United States Department of Agriculture Forest Service (www.fs.usda.gov/detail/fishlake/home/?cid-STELPRDB5393641).

59. Robert Macfarlane. *The secrets of the wood wide web*. The New Yorker, Aug 7, 2016 (www.newyorker.com/tech/annals-of-technology/the-secrets-of-the-wood-wide-web).

60. Valentina Lagomarsino. *Exploring the underground network of trees – the nervous system of the forest*. Harvard University: Science in the News, May 6, 2019 (sitn.hms.harvard.edu/flash/2019/exploring-the-underground-network-of-trees-the-nervous-system-of-the-forest).

61. Johnson & Johnson. *What it's like to be the custodian of Johnson & Johnson's over 130-year history*. Employee Spotlight, Jul 2, 2019 (www.jnj.com/our-heritage/meet-johnson-johnson-chief-historian-margaret-gurowitz).

62. Johnson & Johnson. *Our Story: Our commitment to women* (ourstory.jnj.com/our-commitment-to-women#commitment-to-women).

63. English Heritage. *Slavery connections to English Heritage sites*. English Heritage: Slavery Research (www.english-heritage.org.uk/learn/research/slavery).

64. Henry Mance. *How UK heritage is coming to terms with its links to slavery*. Financial Times, Sep 25, 2020 (www.ft.com/content/ffbfd312-c56b-4b30-8b5d-62b5c9885712).

65. Interview with Dianna Langley and Morgane Bradley, Oxfam International, June 2020.

66. NHS. *Redeployed staff working to beat COVID-19*. North Tees and Hartlepool NHS Foundation Trust, May 21, 2020 (www.nth.nhs.uk/news/redeployed-staff-working-to-beat-covid-19).

67. FeedNHS.com. *Some news and thank yous*. Jun 1, 2020 (www.feednhs.com/some-news-thank-yous).

Habitats

68. Leesman. *The impact of home working on employee experience*. The Insight Group, 2020 (www.hminsightgroup.com/Leesman_HMiller_50k_briefing_130720.pdf).

69. Siemens AG. *Siemens to establish mobile working as core component of the "new normal"*. Press release, Jul 16, 2020 (press.siemens.com/global/en/pressrelease/siemens-establish-mobile-working-core-component-new-normal).

70. Gartner. *Gartner HR survey reveals 41% of employees likely to work remotely at least some of the time post coronavirus pandemic*. Gartner: Newsroom, Apr 14, 2020 (www.gartner.com/en/newsroom/press-releases/2020-04-14-gartner-hr-survey-reveals-41--of-employees-likely-to-).

71. Anne Roderique-Jones. *I practiced hygge and it's kind of the best thing ever*. SELF: Mental Health, Dec 25, 2018 (www.self.com/story/practicing-hygge-danish-lifestyle).

72. Tristan Roberts. *We spend 90% of our time indoors. Says who?* Building Green: Blog post, Dec 15, 2016 (www.buildinggreen.com/blog/we-spend-90-our-time-indoors-says-who).

73. Gabriel Moser, David Uzzell. 'Environmental psychology', in: R Baumeister, KD Vohs, eds. *Encyclopedia of social psychology*. Sage, 2007 (www.researchgate.net/publication/234167386_Environmental_Psychology).

74. Linda Victoria Rolfö. *Relocation to an activity-based flexible office – design processes and outcomes*. Applied Ergonomics, 2018, 73: 141–50 (www.sciencedirect.com/science/article/pii/S0003687018301406).

75. Elizabeth Marsh. *Winner of Digital Workplace Leader of the Year 2019 – Marc Bramoullé at Ubisoft*. DWG: News, Aug 14, 2019 (digitalworkplacegroup.com/2019/08/14/winner-of-digital-workplace-leader-of-the-year-2019-marc-bramoulle-at-ubisoft).

76. Stephen R Kellert. *What is and is not biophilic design?* Metropolis, Oct 2016 (www.metropolismag.com/architecture/what-is-and-is-not-biophilic-design).

77. Gensler Research Institute. *Experience Index*. Gensler: Research & Insight (www.gensler.com/research-insight/gensler-research-institute/experience-index).

78. Ethan Bernstein, Ben Waber. *The truth about open offices*. Harvard Business Review: Collaboration, Nov–Dec 2019 (hbr.org/2019/11/the-truth-about-open-offices).

79. Varsha Saha. *50 expert warehouse design and layout ideas and tips*. Camcode: Industry Resources Blog, Jun 23, 2020 (www.camcode.com/asset-tags/warehouse-design-and-layout-tips).

80. Nicola J Millard. *Productivity, the digital workplace and the collaboration conundrum*. BT: SlideShare (www.slideshare.net/NMillard/productivity-the-digital-workplace-and-the-collaboration-v2k).

81. Andrew Hill, Emma Jacobs. *How is the world's mass homeworking experiment going?* Financial Times, Mar 29, 2020 (www.ft.com/content/75639ffa-6f95-11ea-89df-41bea055720b).

82. Interview with Ryan Anderson, VP, Global Research & Insights, Herman Miller, July 2020.

83. Anne Cassidy. *Clocking off: The companies introducing nap time to the workplace*. The Guardian: Wellness at Work, Dec 4, 2017 (www.theguardian.com/business-to-business/2017/dec/04/clocking-off-the-companies-introducing-nap-time-to-the-workplace).

84. Matluba Khan. *I redesigned a school playground for my PhD – and the children got better grades learning outside*. The Conversation: Agenda, Jun 12, 2020 (theconversation.com/i-redesigned-a-school-playground-for-my-phd-and-the-children-got-better-marks-learning-outside-131587).

85. Shimrit Janes. *"My city, My office"? The rise of mobile working in and beyond our cities*. DWG: News, Nov 21, 2019 (digitalworkplacegroup.com/2019/11/21/my-city-my-office-the-rise-of-mobile-working-in-and-beyond-our-cities).

86. Paul Miller, Elizabeth Marsh. *Digital workplace 2030: Preparing now for the digital worlds of work to come*. DWG Research, 2018 (digitalworkplacegroup.com/resources/download-reports/digital-workplace-2030-preparing-now-digital-worlds-work-come).

87. CBRE. *Smart Workplace 2040: The rise of the workplace consumer*. CBRE Global Workplace Solutions, 2015 (f.tlcollect.com/fr2/816/52576/Smart_Workplace_2040.pdf).

88. Sophie Charara. *The pandemic will change the way our homes and offices are built*. Wired, Jun 16, 2020 (www.wired.co.uk/article/coronavirus-pandemic-office-homes).

89. Dovas. *Office in Madrid lets employees feel like they're working in the woods*. Bored Panda: Architecture, Interior Design, 2014 (www.boredpanda.com/sustainable-forest-office-madrid-selgascano).

Biodiversity

90. Shimrit Janes. *Nurturing cultures of inclusivity and belonging with the digital workplace*. DWG: News, Jan 22, 2020 (digitalworkplacegroup.com/2020/01/22/nurturing-cultures-of-inclusivity-and-belonging-with-the-digital-workplace).

91. Lincoln Quillian, et al. *Hiring discrimination against black Americans hasn't declined in 25 years*. Harvard Business Review (hbr.org/2017/10/hiring-discrimination-against-black-americans-hasnt-declined-in-25-years).

92. Emma Hinchcliffe. *'You can't choose to walk away': Black women detail their experiences with racism in the workplace*. Fortune, Jul 5, 2020 (fortune.com/2020/07/05/black-women-racism-at-work).

93. Peter Bailinson, et al. *LGBTQ+ voices: Learning from lived experiences*. McKinsey Quarterly, Jun 25, 2020 (www.mckinsey.com/business-functions/organization/our-insights/lgbtq-plus-voices-learning-from-lived-experiences).

94. John Pring. *Disabled people 'badly let down by government' during pandemic, says TUC*. Disability News Service, Sep 17, 2020 (www.disabilitynewsservice.com/disabled-people-badly-let-down-by-government-during-pandemic-says-tuc).

95. Kweilin Ellingrud, Simon London, Lareina Yee. *What you need to know about women at work*. McKinsey Global Institute: Podcast, Oct 24, 2019 (www.mckinsey.com/featured-insights/gender-equality/what-you-need-to-know-about-women-at-work).

96. Alastair Duggin. *Creating the UK government's accessibility empathy lab*. GOV.UK: Government Digital Service blog, Jun 20, 2018 (gds.blog.gov.uk/2018/06/20/creating-the-uk-governments-accessibility-empathy-lab).

97. Laura Morgan Roberts, Courtney L McCluney. *Working from home while Black*. Harvard Business Review, Jun 17, 2020 (hbr.org/2020/06/working-from-home-while-black).

98. Sarah Butler. *'The support never stops' – former prisoner working for Timpson*. The Guardian: Business, Apr 6, 2019 (www.theguardian.com/business/2019/apr/06/the-support-never-stops-says-prisoner-who-works-at-timpsons).

99. Damian Carrington. *What is biodiversity and why does it matter to us?* The Guardian: Briefing, Mar 12, 2018 (www.theguardian.com/news/2018/mar/12/what-is-biodiversity-and-why-does-it-matter-to-us).

100. AXA. *Biodiversity at risk: Preserving the natural world for our future*. AXA Research Guide (www.axa-research.org/en/news/biodiversity-at-risk-preserving-the-natural-world-for-our-future).

101. Lisa Feldkamp. *Maintaining healthy forests takes more than planting trees*. Cool Green Science, Aug 2, 2016 (blog.nature.org/science/2016/08/02/maintaining-healthy-forests-takes-more-than-planting-trees).

102. Shimrit Janes. *How to encourage and measure impactful digital collaboration*. DWG: News, Jul 24, 2019 (digitalworkplacegroup.com/2019/07/24/how-to-encourage-and-measure-impactful-digital-collaboration).

103. Janice Gassam Asare. *How to retain diverse talent*. Forbes, Sep 26, 2018 (www.forbes.com/sites/janicegassam/2018/09/26/how-to-retain-diverse-talent/#373798352d33).

104. Steve Bynghall. *Richemont's global intranet*. DWG: Digital Workplace Live, Feb 15, 2018 (members.digitalworkplacegroup.com/blogpost/439672/294880/Digital-Workplace-Live-recording-Richemont-s-global-intranet?).

Sources

All urls correct at time of going to print, November 2020.

[105] Katherine W Phillips. *How diversity makes us smarter*. Scientific American, Oct 1, 2014 (www.scientificamerican.com/article/how-diversity-makes-us-smarter).

[106] Courtney L McCluney, et al. *The costs of codeswitching*. Harvard Business Review: Advancing Black Leaders, Nov 15, 2019 (hbr.org/2019/11/the-costs-of-codeswitching).

[107] Shimrit Janes. *Understanding the relationship between organizational culture and the digital workplace*. DWG Research, 2015 (digitalworkplacegroup.com/resources/download-reports/understanding-the-relationship-between-organizational-culture-and-the-digital-workplace).

[108] Jonny Gifford, et al. *Diversity management that works: An evidence-based review*. Research report, University of Westminster for CIPD, Oct 2019 (www.cipd.co.uk/Images/7926-diversity-and-inclusion-report-revised_tcm18-65334.pdf).

[109] Inditex. *How we do business: Our suppliers* (www.inditex.com/web/guest/comprometidos-con-las-personas/nuestros-proveedores).

[110] Katherine W Phillips, et al. *Better decisions through diversity*. Kellogg School of Management at Northwestern University: Kellogg Insight, Oct 1, 2010 (insight.kellogg.northwestern.edu/article/better_decisions_through_diversity).

[111] Eskalara. *Inclusion benefits everyone*. Eskalara blog, Jun 6, 2019 (eskalera.com/2019/06/06/inclusion-benefits-everyone).

[112] Satya Nadella. *Coming together to combat COVID-19*. LinkedIn, Mar 21, 2020 (www.linkedin.com/pulse/coming-together-combat-covid-19-satya-nadella).

[113] Shimrit Janes. *Collaborating in the digital workplace: How to have and to measure impact*. DWG Research, 2019 (digitalworkplacegroup.com/resources/download-reports/collaborating-in-the-digital-workplace-how-to-have-and-to-measure-impact).

[114] Ruth Holmes. *'Keep flexible work practices post-COVID': New campaign*. Relocate Global, Jun 19, 2020 (www.relocatemagazine.com/news/hr-talent-management-covid-keep-flexible-work-practices-post-covid-new-campaign-rholmes-0620).

[115] Meg Bolger. *What's the difference between diversity, inclusion, and equity?* General Assembly Blog: Social impact, May 24, 2020 (generalassemb.ly/blog/diversity-inclusion-equity-differences-in-meaning).

[116] Dow. *Inclusion & Diversity, 2020* (corporate.dow.com/en-us/about/company/beliefs-and-culture/diversity.html).

[117] Fiona Hathorn. *How will Covid-19 impact diversity in UK business?* Board Agenda, May 28, 2020 (boardagenda.com/2020/05/28/how-will-COVID-19-impact-diversity-in-uk-business).

Relationships

[118] Steve Bynghall. *Connected companies with Workplace from Facebook*. DWG Technology and Research Institute, May 22, 2020 (members.digitalworkplacegroup.com/blogpost/439672/348403/DWG-Technology-and-Research-Institute-Technology-Exchange-recording-Connected-companies-with-Workplace-from-Facebook?).

[119] Sunnyscope. *Symbiotic relationships of the bird world*. Sunnyscope: Nature, May 15, 2018 (www.sunnysports.com/blog/symbiotic-relationships-bird-world).

[120] Evie Wright. *Hunting school for orcas*. BBC Two: Patagonia – Earth's secret paradise (www.bbc.co.uk/programmes/articles/5CwGj57DFpzW1G3Tq0hb607/hunting-school-for-orcas).

[121] Matt Walker. *Why nest-building penguins turn to a life of crime*. BBC Earth: Attenborough's Story of Life, Dec 15, 2016 (www.bbc.com/earth/story/20161214-criminal-penguins-steal-stones).

[122] Liz Langley. *We couldn't have figs without wasps. Here's how mutualism works*. National Geographic, Sep 25, 2020 (www.nationalgeographic.com/animals/reference/mutualism).

[123] Estelle Hakner. *13 amazing otter facts*. Discover Wildlife (www.discoverwildlife.com/animal-facts/mammals/facts-about-otter).

[124] The Career Innovation Company. *Reverse mentoring case study*. Ci 'Digital Generation Initiative': Case studies (www.careerinnovation.com/publications/reverse-mentoring-case-study).

[125] Donald McBryde. *Digital Friends mentoring celebrates 100 partnerships*. Scottish Government: Digital Engagement, Nov 28, 2018 (blogs.gov.scot/digital-engagement/2018/11/28/digital-friends-mentoring-celebrates-100-partnerships).

[126] Interview with Dr Nicola Millard, Principal Innovation Partner, BT, July 2020.

[127] Kuang-Yuan Huang, et al. *Web 2.0 use and organizational innovation: A knowledge transfer enabling perspective*. Association for Information Systems Electronic Library (AISeL), Aug 2010 (aisel.aisnet.org/cgi/viewcontent.cgi?article=1181&context=amcis2010).

[128] Matt Mullenweg. *The importance of meeting in-person*. Automattic, Oct 16, 2018 (ma.tt/2018/10/the-importance-of-meeting-in-person).

[129] Demet Dagdelen. *How communication density fuels Automattic*. Data for Breakfast, Aug 8, 2017 (data.blog/2017/08/08/how-communication-density-fuels-automattic).

[130] Mark Adams. *The road to Royal Leamington Spa: Arrival*. Vitsoe, Oct 16, 2017 (www.vitsoe.com/rw/voice/arrival).

[131] WHY Magazine. *Work life* (www.hermanmiller.com/stories/why-magazine/work-life).

[132] Sam Marshall. *Hubs, hives, and hangouts: Adapting your digital workplace*. ClearBox Consulting, Sep 6, 2016 (www.clearbox.co.uk/hubs-hives-and-hangouts-adapting-your-digital-workplace).

[133] Microsoft (img-prod-cms-rt-microsoft-com.akamaized.net/cms/api/am/imageFileData/RWs2cN?).

[134] PESTLEanalysis Contributor. *How STEEP and STEEPLE analysis help in business*. PESTLE Analysis, Feb 13, 2015 (pestleanalysis.com/steep-and-steeple-analysis).

[135] Kate Raworth. *What on earth is the doughnut?* Exploring doughnut economics (www.kateraworth.com/doughnut).

Structures

[136] Barclays. *Digital Eagles: Build your digital skills with us* (www.barclays.co.uk/digital-confidence/eagles/#:~:text=In%20April%202013%2C%2018%20colleagues,help%20improve%20their%20digital%20skills).

[137] DWG. *Digitally transforming two of the world's oldest banks*. Digital Workplace Impact podcast, Ep 7, 2017 (digitalworkplacegroup.com/dwg_podcast/digitally-transforming-worlds-oldest-banks).

[138] RSPB. *Starling murmurations*. Royal Society for the Protection of Birds: Birds & Wildlife (www.rspb.org.uk/birds-and-wildlife/wildlife-guides/bird-a-z/starling/starling-murmurations).

[139] Smithsonian. *Bait ball*. Ocean: Find Your Blue (ocean.si.edu/ocean-life/fish/bait-ball).

[140] Thomas P Peschak. *Swimming inside a 'fish tornado'*. National Geographic, Sep 18, 2017 (www.nationalgeographic.com/photography/proof/2017/09/trevally-school-peschak).

[141] MAAREC. *The colony and its organization*. Mid-Atlantic Apiculture Research and Extension Consortium (agdev.anr.udel.edu/maarec/honey-bee-biology/the-colony-and-its-organization).

[142] Emily Singer. *The remarkable self-organization of ants*. Quanta Magazine: Biology, Apr 9, 2014 (www.quantamagazine.org/ants-build-complex-structures-with-a-few-simple-rules-20140409).

[143] Mehdi Moussaïd. Twitter: @MehdiMoussaid (twitter.com/Mehdi_Moussaid/status/1221728634760781824).

[144] Janis Dickinson. *Animal social behaviour*. Britannica (www.britannica.com/topic/animal-social-behaviour/The-range-of-social-behaviour-in-animals).

[145] Melissa Hogenboom. *In the frigid Antarctic winter, emperor penguins get too hot*. BBC: Earth, Nov 7, 2015 (www.bbc.co.uk/earth/story/20151107-how-penguins-avoid-overheating).

[146] David Brindle. *Buurtzorg: The Dutch model of neighbourhood care that is going global*. The Guardian, May 9, 2017 (www.theguardian.com/social-care-network/2017/may/09/buurtzorg-dutch-model-neighbourhood-care).

[147] Christine Ro. *Dunbar's number: Why we can only maintain 150 relationships*. BBC Future, Oct 9, 2019 (www.bbc.com/future/article/20191001-dunbars-number-why-we-can-only-maintain-150-relationships).

[148] National Action Plans on Business and Human Rights. *Small & medium-sized enterprises* (globalnaps.org/issue/small-medium-enterprises-smes).

[149] Ayesha Gulzar. *Impact of Industrial Revolution on management thought*. Sukkur IBA Journal of Management and Business, 2(1): 2015 (doi.org/10.30537/sijmb.v2i1.85).

[150] Peter Jacobs, et al. *ING's agile transformation*. McKinsey Quarterly, Jan 10, 2017 (www.mckinsey.com/industries/financial-services/our-insights/ings-agile-transformation).

[151] Joost Minnaar. *The world's most pioneering company of our times*. Corporate Rebels: Bucket List (corporate-rebels.com/haier).

[152] Pim de Morree. *RenDanHeYi: The organizational model defining the future of work?* Corporate Rebels: Forum 2019 (corporate-rebels.com/rendanheyi-forum).

[153] FirstBuild. *Who we are*. Firstbuild.com (firstbuild.com/about).

[154] Caitlin Rosenthal. *Big data in the age of the telegraph*. McKinsey & Company: Organization, Mar 1, 2013 (www.mckinsey.com/business-functions/organization/our-insights/big-data-in-the-age-of-the-telegraph).

[155] Michael Bazigos, et al. *Why agility pays*. McKinsey & Company: Organization, Dec 1, 2015 (www.mckinsey.com/business-functions/organization/our-insights/why-agility-pays).

[156] Wouter Aghina, et al. *The five trademarks of agile organizations*. McKinsey & Company: Organization, Jan 22, 2018 (www.mckinsey.com/business-functions/organization/our-insights/the-five-trademarks-of-agile-organizations).

[157] Boundaryless. *John Bunch – Building complex organizations through simple constraints: Zappos*. Soundcloud: Platform Design Toolkit podcast, Ep 18, Jul 2020 (soundcloud.com/boundaryless-pdt/ep18-john-bunch-building-complex-organizations-through-simple-constraints-zappos).

[158] Liberty Mutual Insurance. *Liberty Mutual Group creates Workgrid Software, LLC to provide business software solutions for mid- to large-sized companies*. About Liberty Mutual (www.libertymutualgroup.com/about-lm/news/articles/liberty-mutual-group-creates-workgrid-software-llc-provide-business-software-solutions-mid-large-sized-companies).

[159] Workgrid. *The Intelligent Workplace Platform* (www.workgrid.com).

[160] Kirkby Diamond. *Vodafone O2 create new company*. CTIL, Oct 15, 2012 (www.kirkbydiamond.co.uk/News/vodafone-O2-create-new-company-CTIL).

[161] LLB reporter. *Telefónica UK and Vodafone network partnership*. London Loves Business, Jan 23, 2019 (londonlovesbusiness.com/telefonica-uk-and-vodafone-network-partnership).

162. The Unilever Foundry. *Unilever's platform for partnering with start-ups to accelerate innovation on a global scale* (www.theunileverfoundry.com).

163. Annabel Beales. *How can partnerships create rapid innovation during COVID-19 crisis?* Business Fights Poverty: Partnerships, May 27, 2020 (businessfightspoverty.org/articles/how-can-partnerships-create-rapid-innovation-during-COVID-19-crisis-2).

Life cycles

164. Alexandra Barokova. *The history of the Nokia Company.* GRIN: Seminar paper, 2012 (www.grin.com/document/340144).

165. Natalie Angier. *Do animals grieve over death like we do?* New York Times: Health, Sep 2, 2008 (www.nytimes.com/2008/09/02/health/02iht-02angi.15827535.html).

166. TRVST. *The life cycle of plastic.* TRVST website: Inspiration (www.trvst.world/inspiration/understanding-the-life-cycle-of-plastic).

167. SOM. *B&Q and ageing workers.* Society of Occupational Medicine (www.som.org.uk/bq-and-ageing-workers).

168. Wikipedia. *Veneration of the dead* (en.wikipedia.org/wiki/Veneration_of_the_dead).

169. Bruce N Pfau. *What do millennials really want at work? The same things the rest of us do.* Harvard Business Review: Generational Issues, Apr 7, 2016 (hbr.org/2016/04/what-do-millennials-really-want-at-work?).

170. Natalia Autenrieth. *6 signs of ageism in the workplace – and how to best handle it.* TopResume (www.topresume.com/career-advice/signs-of-ageism-in-the-workplace).

171. Recruiting Times. *Bosses are avoiding hiring women of childbearing age.* Recruiting Times: Legal News, Aug 17, 2018 (recruitingtimes.org/recruitment-and-hr-legal-updates/23898/bosses-are-avoiding-hiring-women-of-childbearing-age).

172. Rachel Muller-Heyndyk. *Workplace period stigma must be tackled.* HR Magazine, May 29, 2019 (www.hrmagazine.co.uk/article-details/workplace-period-stigma-must-be-tackled).

173. Louron Pratt. *McDonald's launches app to enhance education benefits for US staff.* Employee Benefits, Jan 28, 2020 (employeebenefits.co.uk/mcdonalds-launches-app-to-enhance-education-benefits-for-us-staff).

174. McDonald's. *Management degree opportunities* (people.mcdonalds.co.uk/early-career-opportunities/management-degree-apprenticeship-programme/programme).

175. Steve Bynghall. *Nice employee and peer recognition feature on the intranet homepage at Duke Energy.* DWG extranet: Community blogs, Jul 12, 2018 (members.digitalworkplacegroup.com/blogpost/553709/303025/Nice-employee-and-peer-recognition-feature-on-the-intranet-homepage-at-Duke-Energy).

176. Sarah Laskow. *How retirement was invented.* The Atlantic: Business, Oct 24, 2014 (www.theatlantic.com/business/archive/2014/10/how-retirement-was-invented/381802).

177. Kevin Olp. *Employee experience: How digital workplace teams can enhance the employee journey.* DWG Research, 2020 (members.digitalworkplacegroup.com/blogpost/445048/348833/New-DWG-Research-report-Employee-experience-How-digital-workplace-teams-can-enhance-the-employee-journey).

178. Holly Corbett. *How companies are supporting working parents in the COVID economy.* Forbes: Diversity and Inclusion, Jul 30, 2020 (www.forbes.com/sites/hollycorbett/2020/07/30/how-companies-are-supporting-working-parents-in-the-covid-economy/#1715747f328f).

179. Richard Watson. *Why companies die.* Imperial College Business School (www.imperial.ac.uk/business-school/blogs/executive-education/why-companies-die).

180. Nicolaus Li. *Kodak stock surges 1,500% after shift to pharmaceuticals amidst COVID-19.* Hypebeast: Tech, Jul 30, 2020 (hypebeast.com/2020/7/kodak-pharma-shift-1500-percent-stock-surge-info).

181. UN News. *Nearly half of global workforce at risk as job losses increase due to COVID-19: UN labour agency.* UN News: Economic Development, Apr 28, 2020 (news.un.org/en/story/2020/04/1062792).

182. Steve Bynghall. *Harnessing the creativity of your workforce: How digital workplaces facilitate innovation.* DWG Research, 2020 (digitalworkplacegroup.com/resources/download-reports/harnessing-the-creativity-of-your-workforce-how-digital-workplaces-facilitate-innovation).

183. Danielle Romano. *Hershey in midst of a digital transformation.* Convenience Store News, Oct 17, 2018 (csnews.com/hershey-midst-digital-transformation).

184. Sarah Butler, Zoe Wood. *Suffering John Lewis stands at a crossroads on the high street.* The Guardian, Sep 19, 2020 (www.theguardian.com/business/2020/sep/19/suffering-john-lewis-stands-at-a-crossroads-on-the-high-street).

Migration

185. Britannica. *Patterns and processes influencing the structure of marine assemblages* (www.britannica.com/science/marine-ecosystem/Patterns-and-processes-influencing-the-structure-of-marine-assemblages#ref588530).

186. John H Rappole. 'The importance of forest for the world's migratory bird species', in RM deGraaf, RI Miller, eds. *Conservation of faunal diversity in forested landscapes,* pp.389–406, Chapman & Hall, 1996 (link.springer.com/chapter/10.1007/978-94-009-1521-3_13).

187. Carolina Herrera. *Reviving a rainforest helps keep migratory birds' winter home wild.* NRDC: Expert blog, Nov 29, 2012 (www.nrdc.org/experts/carolina-herrera/reviving-rainforest-helps-keep-migratory-birds-winter-home-wild).

188. NASA. *Changes since the last Ice Age.* Earth Observatory, Aug 20, 2002 (earthobservatory.nasa.gov/features/BorealMigration/boreal_migration3.php).

189. Josh Hrala. *Here's how entire forests can migrate to better environments.* Science Alert, Dec 5, 2016 (www.sciencealert.com/the-weird-way-forests-can-migrate).

190. Craig Welch. *Half of all species are on the move – and we're feeling it.* National Geographic, April 27, 2017 (www.nationalgeographic.com/news/2017/04/climate-change-species-migration-disease).

191. Cornell University. *Greatest threat to Eastern forest birds is habitat loss on wintering grounds.* Science Daily: Science News, Jul 24, 2017 (www.sciencedaily.com/releases/2017/07/170724155603.htm).

192. DW.com. *Hedgehogs threatened by loss of habitat and food in Europe.* DW.com: News (www.dw.com/en/hedgehogs-threatened-by-loss-of-habitat-and-food-in-europe/a-48663491).

193. Erin Blakemore. *Human migration sparked by wars, disasters, and now climate.* National Geographic, Mar 1, 2019 (www.nationalgeographic.co.uk/environment/2019/03/human-migration-sparked-wars-disasters-and-now-climate).

194. Brian Handwerk. *Twelve epic migratory journeys animals take every spring.* Smithsonian Magazine, Apr 19, 2019 (www.smithsonianmag.com/science-nature/twelve-epic-migratory-journeys-animals-take-every-spring-180972001).

195. IOM. *World Migration Report 2020.* International Organization for Migration, 2020 (www.un.org/sites/un2.un.org/files/wmr_2020.pdf).

196. Jilll Ella. *Cadbury: The legacy in Birmingham.* BBC Birmingham, Dec 15, 2009 (news.bbc.co.uk/local/birmingham/hi/people_and_places/history/newsid_8412000/8412655.stm).

197. Francesco Castelli. *Drivers of migration: Why do people move?* Journal of Travel Medicine, 2018. 25(1) (doi.org/10.1093/jtm/tay040 (academic.oup.com/jtm/article/25/1/tay040/5056445).

198. BBC News. *Coronavirus: The world in lockdown in maps and charts.* Apr 6, 2020 (www.bbc.co.uk/news/world-52103747).

199. Natalie Whittle. *Welcome to the 15-minute city.* Financial Times, Jul 17, 2020 (www.ft.com/content/c1a53744-90d5-4560-9e3f-17ce06aba69a).

200. Karen Weise. *Microsoft pledges $500 million for affordable housing in Seattle area.* New York Times: Technology, Jan 16, 2019 (www.nytimes.com/2019/01/16/technology/microsoft-affordable-housing-seattle.html).

201. E Tammy Kim. *Microsoft cannot fix Seattle's housing crisis.* New York Times: Opinion, Jan 18, 2019 (www.nytimes.com/2019/01/18/opinion/microsoft-seattle-housing.html).

202. Adam Vaughan, Dominic Rushe. *Starbucks vows to hire 10,000 refugees as US companies condemn Trump travel ban.* The Guardian, Jan 30, 2017 (www.theguardian.com/business/2017/jan/30/trump-travel-ban-starbucks-hire-10000-refugees).

203. IKEA Foundation. *Our commitments to support refugees on the path to self-reliance.* Special Initiatives & Emergency Response, Dec 16, 2019 (ikeafoundation.org/story/our-commitments-to-support-refugees-on-the-path-to-self-reliance).

204. Alison Doyle. *How long should an employee stay at a job?* The Balance Careers, Nov 8, 2019 (www.thebalancecareers.com/how-long-should-an-employee-stay-at-a-job-2059796).

205. Katie Hope. *How long should you stay in one job?* BBC News: Business, Feb 1, 2017 (www.bbc.co.uk/news/business-38828581).

206. Japan Institute for Labour Policy and Training. 'Human resource management', in: *Labor situation in Japan and its analysis: General overview 2015/2016* (www.jil.go.jp/english/lsj/general/2015-2016/3-1.pdf).

207. Amy Adkins. *Millennials: The job-hopping generation.* Gallup: Business Journal (www.gallup.com/workplace/231587/millennials-job-hopping-generation.aspx).

208. US Bureau of Labor Statistics. *Number of jobs, labor market experience, and earnings growth: Results from a national longitudinal survey summary.* Economic News Release, Aug 22, 2019 (www.bls.gov/news.release/nlsoy.nr0.htm).

209. Oliver Staley. *Who says talent development has to stop when an employee moves on?* Quartz at Work, Dec 6, 2018 (qz.com/work/1444592/alumni-programs).

210. Microsoft Alumni Network (www.microsoftalumni.com).

211. Steve Bynghall. *Creating an internal recruitment site with Anthem.* DWG: Digital Workplace Live, Apr 15, 2019 (members.digitalworkplacegroup.com/blogpost/439672/321965/Digital-Workplace-Live-recording-Creating-an-internal-recruitment-site-with-Anthem?).

212. WeWork. *A creative office solution boosts Microsoft's employee productivity.* Ideas by WeWork, Aug 12, 2019 (www.wework.com/ideas/growth-innovation/microsoft-productivity-wework).

213. Chris Locke. *Redundancies looming? It's time to think startup not just outplacement.* HR Director, Jul 26, 2020 (www.thehrdirector.com/features/COVID/making-redundancies-its-time-to-think-startup-not-just-outplacement).

Sources

All urls correct at time of going to print, November 2020.

Threats

214. Jack Nicas. *Apple reaches $2 trillion, punctuating big tech's grip.* New York Times, Aug 19, 2020 (www.nytimes.com/2020/08/19/technology/apple-2-trillion.html).

215. Agnes Costa. *The employee communication revolution: Ripping up the rule book at HSBC.* The Gatehouse Blog, Feb 2, 2015 (www.gatehouse.co.uk/the-employee-communication-revolution-ripping-up-the-rule-book-at-hsbc).

216. Sarah Abbott. *Plants can make memories.* Untamed Science (untamedscience.com/biology/plants/plant-memory).

217. Frans de Waal. *The surprising complexity of animal memories.* The Atlantic: Science, Jun 2, 2019 (www.theatlantic.com/science/archive/2019/06/surprising-complexity-animal-memories/589420).

218. Carl Zimmer. *In the fight for survival, it can help to bluff.* New York Times, Dec 27, 2006 (www.nytimes.com/2006/12/27/health/27iht-snspecies.html).

219. Liz Langley. *Here are the best liars in the animal kingdom.* National Geographic, May 20, 2017 (www.nationalgeographic.com/news/2017/05/animals-lying-liars-birds-squid).

220. Frans de Waal *Are we smart enough to know how smart animals are?* Granta Publications, 2017.

221. Lucia F Jacobs. *Memory for cache locations in Merriam's kangaroo rats.* Dept of Psychology, University of Toronto, in Animal Behaviour, 1992, 43: 585–93 (web.archive.org/web/20140826120701/http://jacobs.berkeley.edu/test/publications/Jacobs_AB92%281%29.PDF).

222. Rafal Stryjek, et al. *Wild Norway rats do not avoid predator scents when collecting food in a familiar habitat: A field study.* Scientific Reports, 8: 9475, Jun 21, 2018 (www.nature.com/articles/s41598-018-27054-4).

223. Mitchell Grant. *Strength, weakness, opportunity and threat (SWOT) analysis.* Investopedia: Fundamental Analysis, Feb 24, 2020 (www.investopedia.com/terms/s/swot.asp).

224. SMG/CMS Wire. *State of Digital Customer Experience Report – 2019* (www.cmswire.simplermedia.com/cw-cp-smg-2019-dcx-report.html).

225. Hitesh Bhasin. *What is Steeple analysis? Meaning and factors.* Marketing91, Mar 6, 2020 (www.marketing91.com/steeple-analysis).

226. DWG. *A sneak peek at what's coming for DWG24: Stagecoach Blink overview.* DWG24 blog posts, Sep 23, 2020 (digitalworkplacegroup.com/2020/09/23/a-sneak-peek-at-whats-coming-for-dwg24).

227. DWG. *How technology is 'renovating' the Home of Cricket.* Digital Workplace Impact podcast, Ep 27, 2018 (digitalworkplacegroup.com/dwg_podcast/renovating-home-cricket).

228. Jessica Clark. *Coronavirus curfew would 'devastate' hospitality industry, experts warn.* City A.M., Sep 16, 2020 (www.cityam.com/coronavirus-curfew-would-devastate-hospitality-industry-experts-warn).

229. Martin Fullard. *Why has the events industry been left behind?* Conference News: Coronavirus Updates, Jul 10, 2020 (www.conference-news.co.uk/coronavirus-updates-blogs/long-read-why-has-events-industry-been-left-behind).

230. Maddy Shaw Roberts. *Musicians express fury as arts jobs not 'viable' in COVID-19 economy.* Classic FM: News, Sep 28, 2020 (www.classicfm.com/music/news/coronavirus/anger-music-arts-jobs-not-viable-rishi-sunak-scheme).

231. Elizabeth Becker. *How hard will the coronavirus hit the travel industry?* National Geographic: Travel, Apr 2, 2020 (www.nationalgeographic.com/travel/2020/04/how-coronavirus-is-impacting-the-travel-industry).

232. DWG. *How COVID-19 showed the true digital power of Duke Energy.* Digital Workplace Impact podcast, Ep 66, 2020 (digitalworkplacegroup.com/dwg_podcast/episode-66-how-COVID-19-showed-the-true-digital-power-of-duke-energy).

Regeneration

233. BMW Group. *The BMW Vision iNEXT: Future focused.* BMW Group: Innovation (www.bmwgroup.com/en/innovation/bmw-vision-i-next.html).

234. BMW Group. *The next 100 years.* PressClub Global, Oct 11, 2016 (www.press.bmwgroup.com/global/article/detail/T0264644EN/bmw-group-the-next-100-years?language=en).

235. Isabella Tree. *Wilding: The return of nature to a British farm.* Picador, 2018.

236. Jessica Clark. *Brewdog to plant 1m trees in £30m ambition to be carbon negative.* City A.M., Aug 27, 2020 (www.cityam.com/brewdog-to-plant-1m-trees-in-30m-ambition-to-be-carbon-negative).

237. India Block. *BrewDog goes carbon negative with wind-powered breweries.* DeZeen, Aug 25, 2020 (www.dezeen.com/2020/08/25/brewdog-carbon-negative-wind-powered-breweries-forest-news).

238. Joshua Rapp Learn. *Complete axolotl genome could reveal the secret of regenerating tissues.* Smithsonian Magazine (www.smithsonianmag.com/science-nature/complete-axolotl-genome-could-reveal-secret-regenerating-tissues-180971335).

239. Kurt Pepanshek. *Wildfires show how climate change is transforming national parks.* National Geographic: Travel, Oct 14, 2020 (www.nationalgeographic.com/travel/2020/10/wildfires-a-sign-climate-change-effects-are-worsening-in-national-parks).

240. Luba Mullen. *How trees survive and thrive after a fire.* National Forest Foundation, Summer/Fall 2017 (www.nationalforests.org/our-forests/your-national-forests-magazine/how-trees-survive-and-thrive-after-a-fire).

241. Government of Canada. *Why forests need fires, insects and diseases.* Aug 8, 2020 (www.nrcan.gc.ca/our-natural-resources/forests-forestry/wildland-fires-insects-disturban/why-forests-need-fires-insects-and-diseases/13081).

242. Rewilding Europe. *What is rewilding?* (rewildingeurope.com/what-is-rewilding).

243. Fiona Harvey. *England's first wild beavers for 400 years allowed to live on River Otter.* The Guardian, Aug 6, 2020 (www.theguardian.com/environment/2020/aug/06/englands-first-wild-beavers-for-400-years-allowed-to-live-on-river-otter).

244. Ben Goldfarb. *How beavers became North America's best firefighter.* National Geographic: Animals, Sep 22, 2020 (www.nationalgeographic.com/animals/2020/09/beavers-firefighters-wildfires-california-oregon).

245. Lu Ying. *Why the new model of business is regenerative by design.* Medium.com, Aug 11, 2020 (medium.com/circularity/why-the-new-model-of-business-is-regenerative-by-design-c2d16cc84f58).

246. Johnny Davis. *How Lego clicked: The super brand that reinvented itself.* The Guardian, Jun 4, 2017 (www.theguardian.com/lifeandstyle/2017/jun/04/how-lego-clicked-the-super-brand-that-reinvented-itself).

247. Scott Anthony, et al. *The top 20 business transformations of the last decade.* Harvard Business Review: Leadership & Managing People, Sep 24, 2019 (hbr.org/2019/09/the-top-20-business-transformations-of-the-last-decade).

248. Daniel Christian Wahl. *Beyond sustainability? – We are living in the century of regeneration.* Medium.com, Apr 8, 2018 (medium.com/@designforsustainability/beyond-sustainability-we-are-living-in-the-century-of-regeneration-4f2b116a65d1).

249. Anthony Hodgson. *Transformative resilience: A response to the adaptive imperative.* Based on papers written for the Carnegie UK Trust, Investigations of the International Futures Forum, Version 2, Feb 2010 (www.academia.edu/5493454/Transformative_Resilience).

250. John Fullerton. *Regenerative capitalism: How universal principles and patterns will shape our new economy.* Capital Institute: Future of Finance, Apr 2015 (capitalinstitute.org/wp-content/uploads/2015/04/2015-Regenerative-Capitalism-4-20-15-final.pdf).

251. Bill Reed. *Shifting from 'sustainability' to regeneration.* Building Research & Information, 2007, 35(6) (www.tandfonline.com/doi/full/10.1080/09613210701475753).

252. Meredith Dale. *5 weird + wonderful regeneration projects that TUA loves.* The Urban Advisory (www.theurbanadvisory.com/five-wonderful-regeneration-projects).

253. SOIL. *SOIL wins Lush Spring Prize for regenerative sanitation solution.* Sustainable Organic Integrated Livelihoods (www.oursoil.org/springprize).

254. Emily Spaven. *Career pivots in Covid-19 times.* LinkedIn, May 2020 (www.linkedin.com/feed/news/career-pivots-in-COVID-19-times-5149282).

255. Chortle. *Comedy Store goes online.* Apr 21, 2020 (www.chortle.co.uk/news/2020/04/21/45931/comedy_store_goes_online).

256. Brittany Anas. *The clever way this hotel chain plans to stay open during the coronavirus closures.* Forbes: Travel, Mar 31, 2020 (www.forbes.com/sites/brittanyanas/2020/03/31/the-clever-way-this-hotel-chain-plans-to-stay-open-during-the-coronavirus-closures).

257. So So Gay. *About us* (sosogay.store/pages/about-us).

Intelligence

258. Daniel Hurst. *Japan lays groundwork for boom in robot carers.* The Guardian, Feb 6, 2018 (www.theguardian.com/world/2018/feb/06/japan-robots-will-care-for-80-of-elderly-by-2020).

259. Will Dunham. *Potential sign of alien life detected on inhospitable Venus.* Reuters: World News, Sep 14, 2020 (uk.reuters.com/article/uk-space-exploration-venus/potential-sign-of-alien-life-detected-on-inhospitable-venus-idUKKBN2652HG).

260. BBC. *Amazing alien legends and stories from history.* BBC Newsround, Mar 20, 2013 (www.bbc.co.uk/newsround/21849758).

261. Michael W Clune. *I don't believe in aliens anymore.* The Atlantic: Science, Aug 8, 2018 (www.theatlantic.com/science/archive/2018/08/struggling-to-love-a-galaxy-without-aliens/566966).

262. Marc Bekoff. *Spider smarts: Data show their minds extend into their webs.* Psychology Today, Feb 18, 2020 (www.psychologytoday.com/us/blog/animal-emotions/202002/spider-smarts-data-show-their-minds-extend-their-webs).

263. Penguin. *Blue Planet II: 'Seeing a fish use a "tool" for the first time was remarkable'.* Extracts from 'Blue Planet II: A new world of hidden depths. Oct 24, 2017 (www.penguin.co.uk/articles/2017/blue-planet-ii-extract-tusk-fish.html).

264. David Fideler. *Nature's living intelligence.* Kosmos, Spring/Summer 2015 (www.kosmosjournal.org/article/natures-living-intelligence).

265. Marco Daldoss Pirri. *Spirituality, the connection to nature, and the role of shamanic rituals.* Master Thesis, Wageningen University, The Netherlands, Forest and Nature Conservation Policy Group, Jan 31, 2019 (edepot.wur.nl/472319).

266. Bina Venkataraman. *Why you should think about being a good ancestor – and 3 ways to start doing it.* Ideas. TED.com, Aug 27, 2019 (ideas.ted.com/why-you-should-think-about-being-a-good-ancestor-and-3-ways-to-start-doing-it).

267. Roman Krznaric. *The good ancestor: How to think long term in a short-term world.* WH Allen, 2020.

268. Zooniverse. *What is the Zooniverse?* (www.zooniverse.org/about).

269. Interview with Isabel de Clercq, thought leader on connected companies, July 2020.

270. Lynne Peskoe-Yang. *What you can learn from the Solarpunk movement.* Rewire, Nov 23, 2018 (www.rewire.org/learn-solarpunk-movement).

271. Alex Basinski. *You've heard of cyberpunk and steampunk, but what's solarpunk?* Medium.com, Jun 12, 2019 (medium.com/@ajbasinski/youve-heard-of-cyberpunk-and-steampunk-but-what-s-solarpunk-e0e472bd9c9f).

272. Microsoft. *AI for Good* (www.microsoft.com/en-us/ai/ai-for-good).

273. Sideways6. *The AstraZeneca story: A crowd-powered strategy.* Sideways6.com (www.sideways6.com/customers/astrazeneca).

274. Ali Breland. *How white engineers built racist code – and why it's dangerous for black people.* The Guardian, Dec 4, 2017 (www.theguardian.com/technology/2017/dec/04/racist-facial-recognition-white-coders-black-people-police).

275. Josh Simons, Dipayan Ghosh. *Utilities for democracy: Why and how the algorithmic infrastructure of Facebook and Google must be regulated.* Brookings: Report, Aug 2020 (www.brookings.edu/research/utilities-for-democracy-why-and-how-the-algorithmic-infrastructure-of-facebook-and-google-must-be-regulated).

276. Matt Burgess. *The lessons we all must learn from the A-levels algorithm debacle.* Wired, Aug 20, 2020 (www.wired.co.uk/article/gcse-results-alevels-algorithm-explained).

277. Johannes Himmelreich. *The everyday ethical challenges of self-driving cars.* The Conversation, Mar 27, 2018 (theconversation.com/the-everyday-ethical-challenges-of-self-driving-cars-92710).

278. Peter Dizikes. *How many jobs do robots really replace?* MIT News Office, May 4, 2020 (news.mit.edu/2020/how-many-jobs-robots-replace-0504).

279. Josh Simons. *AI, decisions, and business.* Digital Workplace Experience: Harvard University Slideshare, Jun 18, 2019 (www.slideshare.net/dwexperience/keynote-politics-business-and-machine-learning-josh-simons).

280. Jake Silburg, James Manyika. *Notes from the AI frontier: Tackling bias in AI (and in humans).* McKinsey Global Institute, June 2019 (www.mckinsey.com/~/media/mckinsey/featured%20insights/artificial%20intelligence/tackling%20bias%20in%20artificial%20intelligence%20and%20in%20humans/mgi-tackling-bias-in-ai-june-2019.pdf).

281. NeMO-Net. *What is NeMO-Net?* (nemonet.info).

282. Susan Miller. *Game generates training data for supercomputer mapping coral reefs.* GCN, Apr 22, 2020 (gcn.com/articles/2020/04/22/nemo-net-coral-mapping.aspx).

283. CoECI. *NASA Tournament Lab.* NASA, Jul 9, 2020 (www.nasa.gov/coeci/ntl).

284. NASA. *Welcome to NASA Solve.* Aug 28, 2020 (www.nasa.gov/solve/index.html).

285. NASA. *Welcome to NASA@Work.* Jul 9, 2020 (www.nasa.gov/coeci/nasa-at-work).

Health

286. renews.biz. *BlackRock leans into the green.* renews.biz, Jan 14, 2020 (renews.biz/57373/blackrock-leans-into-the-green).

287. Brad Smith. *Microsoft will be carbon negative by 2030.* Microsoft: Official Blog, Jan 16, 2020 (blogs.microsoft.com/blog/2020/01/16/microsoft-will-be-carbon-negative-by-2030).

288. John Elkington. *25 Years ago I coined the phrase "triple bottom line." Here's why it's time to rethink it.* Harvard Business Review: Sustainability, Jun 25, 2018 (hbr.org/2018/06/25-years-ago-i-coined-the-phrase-triple-bottom-line-heres-why-im-giving-up-on-it).

289. Ido Badash, et al. *Redefining health: The evolution of health ideas from antiquity to the era of value-based care.* Cureus, 2017, 9(2): e1018 (www.ncbi.nlm.nih.gov/pmc/articles/PMC5346014).

290. Xinyin Chen, Leora C Swarzman. 'Health beliefs and experiences in Asian cultures', in Shané S Kazarian, David R Evans, eds. *Handbook of cultural health psychology*, Academic Press, 2001, pp.389–410 (www.researchgate.net/publication/290818936_Health_Beliefs_and_Experiences_in_Asian_Cultures).

291. GreenRoofs.com. *ACROS Fukuoka Prefectural International Hall* (www.greenroofs.com/projects/acros-fukuoka-prefectural-international-hall).

292. Edelman. *Edelman Trust Barometer 2020.* Global report, 2020 (cdn2.hubspot.net/hubfs/440941/Trust%20Barometer%202020/2020%20Edelman%20Trust%20Barometer%20Global%20Report.pdf).

293. Steve Bynghall. *Evolving the employee mobile experience: Six key approaches for success.* DWG Research, 2017 (digitalworkplacegroup.com/resources/download-reports/evolving-the-employee-mobile-experience-six-key-approaches-for-success).

294. BT. *People, productivity and the digital workplace: How mobile and collaboration services can boost productivity.* Whitepaper, Mar 8, 2018 (www.globalservices.bt.com/en/insights/whitepapers/people-productivity-in-digital-workplace).

295. V Garrow, et al. *Fish or bird? Perspectives on Organisational Development (OD).* Brighton, Institute for Employment Studies, 2008 (employment-studies.co.uk/system/files/resources/files/463.pdf).

296. Chris Gagnon, et al. *Organizational health: A fast track to performance improvement.* McKinsey & Company, Sep 7, 2017 (www.mckinsey.com/business-functions/organization/our-insights/organizational-health-a-fast-track-to-performance-improvement).

297. New Zealand Government. *The Wellbeing Budget.* NZ Treasury, May 30, 2019 (treasury.govt.nz/sites/default/files/2019-05/b19-wellbeing-budget.pdf).

298. New Zealand Government. *Living Standards Framework – Dashboard.* NZ Treasury (lsfdashboard.treasury.govt.nz/wellbeing).

299. Anne-Marie Bagnall. *Can we measure the wellbeing of a 'community'?* What Works Wellbeing, Aug 9, 2017 (whatworkswellbeing.org/blog/can-we-measure-the-wellbeing-of-a-community).

300. MHFA England. *Being a mental health first aider: Your guide to the role* (mhfaengland.org/remote-working-resources/mental-health-first-aiders).

301. Ashleigh Webber. *Thirty leading companies sign up to mental health commitment.* Personnel Today, Occupational Health and Welbeing, 2019 (www.personneltoday.com/hr/mental-health-at-work-commitment).

302. Technische Universitaet Muenchen. *How do plants grow towards the light? Scientists explain mechanism behind phototropism.* Science Daily, May 28, 2013 (www.sciencedaily.com/releases/2013/05/130528105946.htm)

Reflections

303. Charles Eisenstein. *The more beautiful world our hearts know is possible.* North Atlantic Books, 2013 (charleseisenstein.org/books/the-more-beautiful-world-our-hearts-know-is-possible).

Image credits

Front/back cover: Deciduous forest © Smileus/Shutterstock.com

Copyright page: Hotel Narvil Conference & Spa, Narvil, Poland © Grand Warszawski/Shutterstock.com

Quote page: Metamorphosis of monarch butterfly © Darkdiamond67/Shutterstock.com

Title page: Natural spiral, succulent plant © Harry Clues/Shutterstock.com

Acknowledgements page: Bluebell woods, Oxfordshire, UK © allouphoto/Shutterstock.com

Contents page: Path through forest in autumn © dugdax/Shutterstock.com

2: Sunlight through tree with spectacular roots © Jeremy Bishop/Unsplash

4: Sunflower © Min C Chiu/Shutterstock.com

5: Group of ammonites in stone © URRaL/Shutterstock.com

7: Sustainable oval building, Cologne, Germany © Pixel 8/Alamy

10: Himalayas visible from India during lockdown © Yogesh Kumar Attri/iStock by Getty Images

13–14: Gardens by the Bay, Singapore © timJ/Unsplash

15: Skydiver jumping out of plane © Mauricio Graiki/iStock by Getty Images

18: Plant cell under microscope © Barbol/Shutterstock.com

21: Oak tree seedling © jurgal/Shutterstock.com

23–24: 12 elements illustration by Liad Janes

Purpose:
Apple skin © Radu Marcusu/Unsplash
Roots:
Grass © Bradley Brister/Unsplash
Soil © paul mocan/Unsplash
Habitats:
Snow © Ant Rozetsky/Unsplash
Water © Rodion Kutsaev/Unsplash
Biodiversity:
Sky © Anton Darius/Unsplash
Grass © Claudel Rheault/Unsplash
Leaves © vickholius Nugroho/Unsplash
Water © Geoffrey Baumbach/Unsplash
Relationships:
Ocean © Christian Palmer/Unsplash
Structures:
Plant © Yousef Espanioly/Unsplash
Life cycles:
Leaves © Annie Spratt/Unsplash
Migration:
Snow © Michael Hacker/Unsplash
Tree and grass © Johann Siemens/Unsplash
Threats:
Eagle © Luca Huter/Unsplash
Regeneration:
Autumn leaves © Rin Porter/Unsplash
Intelligence:
Space © Jeremy Thomas/Unsplash
Health:
Tree © Jeremy Bishop/Unsplash

Background image:
White and brown concrete spiral stairs © Dan Freeman/Unsplash

25–26: Oriental pied hornbill, Singapore © Mark Stoop/Unsplash

27–28: Tree roots prevent soil erosion © Apichart Thodrat/123RF.com

29: Schoolchildren protesting on environmental issues © Markus Spiske/Pexels

31–32: Ripples of water © YJ.K./Shutterstock.com

33: Polar bear cubs play fight © Alexey Seafarer/Shutterstock.com

35–36: Tree roots © KhunYing/Shutterstock.com

37: Ancient bristlecone pine, Inyo National Forest, California © Heather Lucia Snow/Shutterstock.com

39–40: Mossman Gorge, Daintree National Park, Queensland, Australia © AustralianCamera/Shutterstock.com

41: Quaking aspens, Vail, Colorado, USA © Colin D Young/Shutterstock.com

43–44: Wood wide web illustration © Macrina Busato

45: Mycorrhizal fungi © Eye of Science/Science Photo Library

47–48: Arctic fox © Ondrej Prosicky/Shutterstock.com

50: Lesser yellownape woodpecker © momnoi/iStock by Getty Images

51: Design for Nautilus Eco-Resort, Biomimetic Learning Centre, Palawan, Philippines © Vincent Callebaut

53–54: Women working in office with plants © Jacob Lund/Shutterstock.com

55–56: Selgascano Madrid Office © Iwan Baan

57: Spiral staircase © C J Dayrit/Unsplash

59–60: Bee on lavendar flower © Heather McKean/Unsplash

61: Dry stone wall, Cornwall © Alison Chapman

64: Coral reef, Red Sea, Egypt © Solarisys/Shutterstock.com

65–66: Wildflower meadow, Carpathian Mountains, Romania © Alex Cofaru/Shutterstock.com

67–68 (top left to bottom right):
Kea, New Zealand © John Yunker/Unsplash
Turtle, Maui, Hawaii © Stephen Leonardi/Unsplash
Blue dragonfly © Shreyas Bhosale/Unsplash
Green snake © Alfonso Castro/Unsplash
Lyle's flying fox © jekjob/Shutterstock.com
Spider © Wynand Uys/Unsplash
Kingfisher © Boris Smokrovic/Unsplash
Red-eyed tree frog © Vaclek Sebek/Shutterstock.com
Panda in tree © Hung Chung Chih/Shutterstock.com
Sally lightfoot crab © Steve Cymro/Shutterstock.com
Rhino © David Clode/Unsplash

Jellyfish, Japan © Ryoji Hayasaka/Unsplash
Koala bear © David Clode/Unsplash
Tiger © Mike Marrah/Unsplash
Orang-utan © Dawn Armfield/Unsplash
Caterpillar © Boris Smokrovic/Unsplash

69: Rainbow over field of dandelions © Aleksandr Ozerov/Shutterstock.com

71–72: Group of meerkats © Mrinal Pal/Shutterstock.com

74: Mare with foal © Erica Hollingshead/Shutterstock.com

75–76: Zebras and ostriches © Artush/iStock by Getty Images

77–78: Family group of monkeys, grooming © Alison Chapman

79–80: Vitsoe UK HQ, Leamington Spa © Dirk Lindner

81: Small-clawed otter juggling a stone © Cloudtail_the_Snow_Leopard/iStock by Getty Images

83–84: Ants working together © frank60/Shutterstock.com

85–86: Emperor penguin huddle © Stefan Christmann/Naturepl.com

87–88: Nautilus seashell © KMNPhoto/Shutterstock.com

89–90: Starling murmuration © Albert Beukhof/Shutterstock.com

91: Three lionesses © Andy Rouse/Naturepl.com

93: Plan of organization, New York and Erie railroad, 1855, courtesy of the Geography and Map Division, Library of Congress

95: Sardine bait ball © Andrea Izzotti/Shutterstock.com

97–98: Three young plants © Innulya/Shutterstock.com

100: Polluted beach © Erlo Brown/Shutterstock

101: Elephants mourning dead baby © brittak/iStock by Getty Images

105–106: Autumn leaves © S.Borisov/Shutterstock.com

107: Fungi growing on tree stump © AleksanderMilutinovic/Shutterstock.com

109–110: Wildebeest migration © Henk Bogaard/Shutterstock.com

112: Monarch butterfly migration © Cathy & Gordon Illg/Janes Gallery/DanitaDelimont.com/Shutterstock.com

113–114: Adelie penguin migration, South Orkneys © Ivan Hoermann/Shutterstock.com

115–116: Common crane migration, Hortobagy National Park, Hungary © Artush/Shutterstock.com

118: Hedgehog crossing road © Serhii Khomiak/Shutterstock.com

119: Red crab migration, Christmas island © Yvonne McKenzie/ Wondrous World Images 2020

121–122: Long-eared owl © Ondrej Prosicky/Shutterstock.com

124: Green chameleon © Michael Held/Unsplash

125–126: Brown rats © Gallinago_media/Shutterstock.com

128: Crown shyness in trees © H-AB Photography/Shutterstock.com

129–130: Wolves © David Dirga/Shutterstock.com

131: Sphinx hawk-moth caterpillar © Mark Bowler/Naturepl.com

133–134: Dead trees, Deadvlei, Namibia © Mike Morash

135: Tamworth pigs, Knepp Estate © Knepp Wildland

136: Jack pine cone © LifeisticAC/Shutterstock.com

137–138: Beaver, Devon Wildlife Trust © Nick Upton/Alamy Stock Photo

139: Reforested hillside, Calima, Colombia © PlataRoncallo/Shutterstock.com

141–142: Public toilet, Kawakawa, New Zealand © Michael Kaercher/Shutterstock.com

143: Axolotl © Arm001/Shutterstock.com

145–146: The Milky Way over a pine forest © Andrey Prokhorov/Shutterstock.com

147–148: *Mimosa pudica* plant © AjayTvm/Shutterstock.com

149–150: Spider web with dew © Meagan Smart/Shutterstock.com

151–152: Futuristic view of Paris © Vincent Callebaut

154: Corals, Japan © Tomoe Steineck/Unsplash

155: Earth seen from space, based on image furnished by NASA © Dima Zel/Shutterstock.com

157–158: Bluebell woods in spring, Oxfordshire, UK © AdamEdwards/Shutterstock.com

159–160: Dead forest by lake, Manasquan Reservoir, New Jersey, USA © Stephen Bonk/Shutterstock.com

161–162: Fukuoka Prefectural International Hall, Kyushu, Japan © MrNovel/Shutterstock.com

163–164: Damselfly on bud © Darkdiamond67/Shutterstock.com

166: Flower turning towards the sun © Witaya Proadtayakogool/Shutterstock.com

167: Health icon, illustration by Liad Janes
Tree © Jeremy Bishop/Unsplash

170: Mawgan Porth beach, Cornwall, UK © Alison Chapman

172: Hillside with biodiversity of wild flowers and forest © bdavid32/Shutterstock.com

180: Looking up at beech tree © Smileus/Shutterstock.com

Index

Note: page numbers in italics refer to illustrations and their captions.

Index

Note: page numbers in italics refer to illustrations and their captions.